P | I

# THE PIG BOOK

G | S

# THE PIG BOOK

## RUSSELL ASH

TIMBRE BOOKS

**ARBOR HOUSE**

**NEW YORK**

**P** | **I**

For My Pigling

Designed by Tony Spalding
Cover design by Frank Phillips

First impression 1986
Copyright © 1985 by Russell Ash

Library of Congress Cataloging-in-Publication Data
Ash, Russell.
The pig book.
1. Swine—Miscellanea.   I.  Title.
SF395.4.A84   1986   636.4   85-13448
ISBN 0-87795-751-7 (pbk.)

Filmset by Advanced Filmsetters (Glasgow) Ltd
Printed in Great Britain at the University Press, Cambridge

**G** | **S**

# CONTENTS

○

## OUR FRIEND, THE PIG 6

T IS PERHAPS HIS SIMILARITY to us that has led to our love/hate relationship with the pig. No animal has been more vilified in words – in our use of such terms of abuse as 'greedy pig' and 'filthy swine' – in art and myth – as a devil-possessed symbol of evil, a vicious boar or an 'unclean' animal – and in our treatment of him – especially his undignified end, his head served on a platter with an apple stuck in his mouth. Yet the pig is also revered as one of man's closest and oldest friends, a helpmate to saints and an object of the affection of children in *This Little Piggy* and other nursery rhymes and in a multitude of stories.

In the piggy miscellany that follows, we meet the pig in history, in mythology and folklore, in art, in language and literature – and in the kitchen, and consider the case for the rehabilitation of the pig as a creature of importance, wonder and love.

# OUR FRIEND, THE PIG

There exists perhaps in all creation no animal which has less justice and more injustice shown him than the pig.

*Sir Francis Bond Head (1793–1875)*

## Pig Haters

Some men there are love not a gaping pig.
*Shakespeare* Merchant of Venice, IV.i

The traditional view of the pig is that it is dirty and greedy:
The Common Boar is, of all other domestic quadrupeds, the most filthy and impure. Its form is clumsy and disgusting and its appetite gluttonous and excessive.
*Thomas Bewick (1753–1828)*

There have even been those who are allergic to pigs:
A learned man told me . . . that he knew one at Antwerp, that would immediately swoon, as oft as a pig was set before him, upon any table where he was present.
*Nathaniel Wanley*
Wonders of the Little World, *1678*

*Pigs might fly? A contented pig attempts an impersonation of Dumbo.*

# THREE BELIEFS ABOUT PIGS REFUTED

◆

### Pigs Are Dirty

Pigs have few major sweat glands. They therefore need water or, if it is not available, mud to wallow in to cool their skins by evaporation. Pig-keepers who have provided pigs with children's paddling pools report that they prefer them to mud. Pigs also tend to keep their sties clean by sleeping in one part and depositing dung as far away from their sleeping quarters as possible.

### Pigs Will Eat Anything

Pigs are actually fussier eaters than most domesticated animals. Observers in ancient times noted the range of foodstuffs the pig will *not* eat, while scientists conducting a recent experiment found that of 243 types of vegetable placed before a pig, it refused 171.

*Pigs are dirty? Well, perhaps they are slightly untidy eaters . . .*

*(Above)* Pigs are not really greedy –
but they do enjoy Christmas dinner, as
this drawing by Ronald Searle shows.
*(Right)* Norman Meredith's
traditional view of the pig as a glutton.

## Pigs Are Stupid

I have observed great sagacity in swine, but the short lives we allow them, and their general confinement, prevent their improvement, which would otherwise probably equal that of the dog.

*Erasmus Darwin* Zoonomia, *1794–96*

Experts on animal behaviour have concluded that the pig is probably the tenth most intelligent animal on earth after the primates, the whale, dolphin and elephant. The dog does not even appear in the top ten, and animal trainers who have worked with pigs have been amazed to discover that they can learn everything a dog can, usually more quickly, and seem to be capable of lateral thinking of a highly advanced degree.

*A prophetic view of the shape of pigs to come: fatter (and even cleverer?) pigs as seen by* Punch *in 1865.*

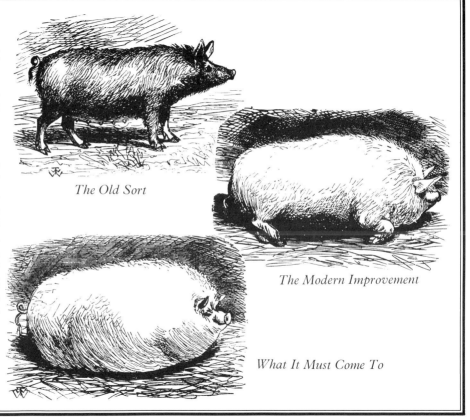

*The Old Sort*

*The Modern Improvement*

*What It Must Come To*

## A Very Sagacious, Artful and Prolific Pig

The natural term of an hog's life is little known, and the reason is plain – because it is neither profitable nor convenient to keep that turbulent animal to the full extent of its time: however, my neighbour, a man of substance, who had no occasion to study every little advantage to a nicety, kept an half-bred Bantam sow, who was as thick as she was long, and whose belly swept on the ground, till she was advanced to her seventeenth year; at which period she showed some tokens of age by the decay of her teeth and the decline of her fertility.

For about ten years this prolific mother produced two litters in the year of about ten at a time, and once above twenty at a litter; but as there were near double the number of pigs to that of teats, many died. From long experience in the world this female was grown very sagacious and artful: when she found occasion to converse with a boar she used to open all the intervening gates, and march, by herself, up to a distant farm where one was kept; and when her purpose was served would return by the same means. At the age of about fifteen her litters began to be reduced to four or five; and such a litter she exhibited when in her fatting-pen. She proved, when fat, good bacon, juicy, and tender; the rind, or sward, was remarkably thin. At a moderate computation she was allowed to have been the fruitful parent of three hundred pigs: a prodigious instance of fecundity in so large a quadruped! She was killed in spring 1775.

*Gilbert White, 1776, letter to Daines Barrington in* The Natural History of Selborne, *1788–89*

*(Left) A wise gnome hitches a lift from an equally artful pig: the phrase 'on the pig's back' means 'lucky'. (Right) A prolific pig.*

# PIG LOVERS

◆

## Taking It For Grunted

I have a friendly feeling towards pigs generally, and consider them the most intelligent of beasts . . . I also like his disposition and attitude to all other creatures, especially man. He is not suspicious, or shrinkingly submissive, like horses, cattle and sheep; nor an impudent, devil-may care like the goat; nor hostile like the goose; nor condescending like the cat; nor a flattering parasite like the dog. He views us from a totally different, a sort of democratic standpoint as fellow citizens and brothers, and takes it for granted, or grunted, that we understand his language.

*W. H. Hudson* The Book of a Naturalist, *1919*

## The Beauty Of The Pig

I never could imagine why pigs should not be kept as pets. To begin with, pigs are very beautiful animals. Those who think otherwise are those who do not look at anything with their own eyes, but only through other people's eyeglasses. The actual lines of a pig (I mean of a really fat pig) are among the loveliest and most luxuriant in nature; the pig has the same great curves, swift and yet heavy, which we see in rushing water or in rolling cloud. Compared to him, the horse, for instance, is a bony, angular, and abrupt animal . . . there is no point of view from which a really corpulent pig is not full of sumptuous and satisfying curves . . . You can examine the pig from the top of an omnibus, from the top of the Monument, from a balloon, or an airship; and as long as he is visible he will be beautiful. In short, he has that fuller, subtler, and more universal kind of shapeliness which the unthinking (gazing at pigs and undistinguished journalists) mistake for a mere absence of shape.

*G. K. Chesterton* The Uses of Diversity, *1920*

*A happy pig taking us, and life, for grunted.*

## French Lard Barons

In the rural Auvergne region of France, an English visitor was recently passing a swineherd when she thought she detected familiar tones in the names he was calling to his pigs. Tuning in more closely, she realised that every pig had been given the name of a character from the TV soap opera, *Dallas*. There was a *cochon* representing everyone from J.R. to Pamela, Miss Elly to Bobby Ewing – each, apparently, with a personality to match.

*(Above) A balletic pig at the bar, '... full of sumptuous and satisfying curves'.*
*(Above right) A well-hoofed sow with her Cartier pig ring.*

**P**IG-LIKE ANIMALS APPEARED on earth some 36 million years ago. The European pig, *Sus scrofa*, is descended from the wild pig and is a relative of such animals as the rhinoceros, hippopotamus, warthog, peccary, tapir, porcupine and hedgehog. Archaeological evidence has shown that not only have domesticated varieties of pig usually existed alongside wild pigs, but they have frequently interbred – particularly in the days when swineherds let their pigs roam in the forests. From about 200 years ago, *Sus scrofa* has also been crossed with the Chinese pig, producing new strains that come to maturity earlier, have high fertility and other attributes.

The great value of the pig is that it is highly adaptable and can be allowed to forage for itself or kept in a pig sty (or pig pen); it is prolific and produces a great quantity of meat that can be prepared in hundreds of different

# MAN AND BEAST

## The Story Of Our Relationship With The Pig

*The captive boar: a 3rd–4th century* AD *Roman mosaic from the Sicilian Imperial Palace.*

ways. Early farmers also found it useful in clearing ground: in fact, the pig has been regarded as a primitive but efficient bulldozer, turning up buried roots and enabling the cultivation of grassland; they have thus often been followed in agricultural development by sheep which acted as 'mowers'. Pigs also dig in seeds with their feet, and in ancient Egypt were used to do so and for threshing by trampling corn.

### The Pig In The Ancient World
There can be no doubt that the pig was highly esteemed in the ancient world, except among those cultures whose dietary laws prohibited the eating of pork. Even where the pig was taboo, exceptions were found – for example in Egypt where pigs might be eaten at certain festivals. Some of the earliest laws had to take account of the ownership of pigs: the Hittite *Code of Laws* stated, 'If a pig goes upon a threshing-floor, or a field, or a

garden, and the owner of the meadow, of the field, or of the garden, smites it so that it die, he shall give it back to its owner; but if he does not give it back, he becomes a thief.'

Pigs and boars featured heavily in the myths and legends and in the superstitions of the cultures of the Middle East – in ancient Persia, for instance, pigs were kept in horses' stables to ward off the evil eye. This was nowhere truer than among the classical Greeks, whose mythology is filled with magical pigs and ferocious boars. There was also a practical reason for their prevalence: the Athenians had few pastures, and so raised pigs. Plato, in his *Republic*, stated that swineherds were as important as bakers – a view at odds with that of certain other cultures, where swineherds were held to be the lowest of the low. It was the Romans who developed the science of breeding, caring for and fattening pigs into a recognised discipline which they

called *porculatio*, and as we shall see the pig played a vital part in Roman gastronomy.

## The Pig In Britain

The European pig was domesticated at the end of the Neolithic period, after about 7000 BC. The ancestors of the domestic pig in Britain were either indigenous wild varieties or domesticated European ones brought over in about 2500 BC. Pigs were probably the first domesticated animals in Ireland, where their economic importance was once emphasised by their description as 'the gentleman that pays the rent'.

In Switzerland, archaeological excavations have revealed the remains of the 'turbary pig' – believed to have been a cross between the domesticated and wild types and which is thought to have been introduced into Britain by the Celts. In Britain, turbary pig remains have been found in Glastonbury. It must have taken several centuries though, before there

was a clear divide between the wild and the domesticated varieties, as in his *Geographica* the Roman writer Strabo warned of pigs in Britain that '. . . live abroad in the woods and are remarkable for their height, strength and swiftness – indeed, it is as dangerous for a stranger to approach them as the wolf'.

## Pannage And Pig Rings

In medieval times, pig owners had the legal right to feed their pigs on acorns and beech nuts, or 'mast', in such areas as the New Forest; this right was known as 'pannage', derived from an Old French word meaning 'to feed'. The Domesday Book, the record begun in 1085 which lists ownership of lands and livestock, contains numerous references to 'pannage for 100 (or more) pigs' – as well as offering some clues to the pig population of England at the time: in the counties of Norfolk, Sussex and Essex alone there were 31,000 pigs.

*Fattening pigs on acorns, from the magnificent* Très Riches Heures du Duc de Berry, c. *1412.*

In the Middle Ages, swineherds were permitted to feed their animals in royal forests from Midsummer Day until 15 January and many illustrations of the period depict October as the month during which swineherds were seen knocking down acorns for their hungry charges. But as pressure on the dwindling forests grew, the pannage months were steadily reduced to 15 days before Michaelmas and 40 days after, then 'from Michaelmas to Martinmas'. Also, as the size of Britain's forests reduced, and it was recognised what damage pigs caused by their rooting, 'pig-ringing' – putting rings through their noses to prevent their uprooting plants – became law, with stiff penalties for offenders. In the Elizabethan age, pig-droving from the Midlands to the forests of Sussex and Hampshire was a major seasonal task, but steadily the massive herds and use of pannage reduced, as the pig's status changed to that of ownership often of a single animal by a rural dweller or 'cottager', with none of the traditional rights once associated with its welfare. In 1816 the parish of Clapham in London issued a directive that no-one was permitted to feed swine on Clapham Common; the days of the forest-roaming pannage-feeding pig were over.

## Pig Colonists

On Christopher Columbus' second voyage (1493–96), he took 8 pigs. According to the historian, Bartolomé de las Casas, Bishop of Chiapa, '...from the increase of these eight pigs have come the pigs found everywhere today in the lands of the Indies, all of which were there and ever will be'. Columbus apparently left the pigs on Haiti and their offspring were taken to the American mainland where some of their descendants still live.

Ironically, Columbus found their relatives were already there – on a later voyage (1502–4) he found peccaries in Jamaica.

## The Cottager's Pig

A pig in almost every cottage sty! That is the infallible mark of a happy people.

*William Cobbett* Rural Rides, *1830*

In England, the pig became progressively a cottager's animal after the 16th century. Feeding and caring for it was very much a family affair, and the nature of its food depended very much on local availability. Gloucester Old Spots, for example, traditionally ate whey from the cheese made in that county; in other areas they might be fed on leftovers from the brewing trade – sometimes causing the spectacle of drunken pigs. In the last quarter of the 18th century the appearance of the Chinese pig in Britain resulted in dramatic changes in the physical appearance of the domesticated pig. Cross-bred with English varieties, it produced the Berkshire and other breeds that have remained enormously popular.

## Seasonal Killing

Shut up a young boar, of a year and a half old, in a little room at harvest home, feeding him with nothing but sweet whey, and giving him every morning clean straw to lie upon, but lay it not thick; so before Christmas he will be sufficiently brawned with continual lying, and prove exceedingly fat, wholesome and sweet.

*Thomas Moufet* Health's Improvement, *1746*

## The Family Pig

In *Lark Rise to Candleford*, Flora Thompson, describing life in rural Oxfordshire a century ago, deals at length with that most important member of the family – the pig. She describes the mixed pleasures of having a pig sty adjacent to their cottage, the involvement of the entire family in the pig's well-being and feeding, all leading up to that most significant date in the calendar, when it was slaughtered:

‘When the pig was fattened – and the fatter the better – the date of execution had to be decided upon. It had to take place during the first two quarters of the moon; for, if the pig was killed when the moon was waning the bacon would shrink in cooking, and they wanted it to ‘plimp up’. The next thing was to engage the travelling pork butcher, or pig-sticker, and, as he was a thatcher by day, he always had to kill after dark, the scene being lighted with lanterns and the fire of burning straw which at a later stage of the proceedings was to singe the bristles of the victim.

The killing was a noisy, bloody business, in the course of which the animal was hoisted to a rough bench that it might bleed thoroughly and so preserve the quality of the meat . . . After the carcase had been singed, the pig-sticker would pull off the detachable, gristly, outer coverings of the toes, known locally as ‘the shoes’, and fling them among the children, who scrambled for them, then sucked and

*One of the family: the cottager's pig and her litter by George Morland.*

gnawed them, straight from the filth of the sty and blackened by fire as they were.

The whole scene, with its mud and blood, flaring lights and dark shadows, was as savage as anything to be seen in an African jungle . . .

It was a time to rejoice, and rejoice they did, with beer flowing freely and the first delicious dish of pig's fry sizzling in the frying pan . . .

Then the housewife 'got down to it', as she said. Hams and sides of bacon were salted, to be taken out of the brine later and hung on the wall near the fireplace to dry. Lard was dried out, hog's puddings were made, and the chitterlings were cleaned and turned three days in succession under running water, according to ancient ritual.

It was a busy time, but a happy one, with the larder full and something over to give away, and all the pride and importance of owning such riches.'

## Pig Population

In his *Rural Rides*, William Cobbett reported on the incidence of pigs in most parts of England; but it was in the county of Hampshire that he noted the densest population:

'A little before the village of Beaulieu . . . we went through a wood, chiefly of beech, and that beech seemingly destined to grow food for pigs, of which we saw, during this day, many thousands. I should think that we saw at least a hundred hogs to one deer. I stopped, at one time, and counted the hogs and pigs just round about me, and they amounted to 140, all within 50 or 60 yards of my horse.'

Cobbett, incidentally, took pigs to Long Island and started a line that continues to the present.

## THE PIG'S ROLE
## IN MOMENTOUS
## HISTORICAL EVENTS

### Founding Fathers –
### And Mothers

In *The Aeneid* the Roman poet Virgil tells the story of a sow with 30 piglets that led Aeneas to the location of city of Lavinium. This seems to have started a fashion for helpful pigs guiding city founders to ideal sites and saints to suitable spots for erecting churches.

Evesham Abbey was said to have been founded where Eof or Eoves, while feeding his pigs, saw a vision of the Virgin Mary.

Baldred, the son of Hudibras, a legendary king of Britons, went to Athens to study, but while he was there he unfortunately caught leprosy, so that when he returned to England he became an outcast and worked as a swineherd. One day he noticed that pigs that wallowed in the mud of a local hot spring were miraculously cured of their various skin diseases. He tried the magic mud on himself, was restored to health and reunited with his family. In 863 BC the town of Bath was founded on the site of the pigs' mud bath, and it subsequently became an important Roman centre. A statue of Baldred was erected in 1699, but so far his piggy advisers are uncommemorated.

Fair play is more evident in the 19th century pig monument in Lüneburg, Germany. It consisted of a glass case with a preserved ham in it and a black marble slab with the message, 'Passerby, contemplate here the mortal remains of the pig which acquired for itself imperishable glory by the discovery of the salt springs of Lüneburg'.

## Death Of A Prince

Heir to the French throne, Crown Prince Philippe, son of King Louis VI ('Louis the Fat'), was killed when a pig tripped his horse.

## The Pig That Saved A City

In 1643 during the English Civil War, the city of Gloucester was under siege by a 30,000-strong royalist army encamped in Tredworth Field. Out of ammunition and food, a plan was formulated whereby the last remaining pig was walked around the city and made to squeal so that the king's spies were convinced that the city had hundreds of pigs and could thus hold out for months. On 5 September the royalist army broke camp and marched away. The siege was raised and the City of Gloucester praised the pig who, sad to relate, did not survive his ordeal.

## The Indian Mutiny

In the golden years of the Indian Raj, sepoys (native Indian soldiers) were issued with cartridges for their newly-introduced breech-loading Enfield rifles. Due to an oversight on the part of the munitions factory that supplied them, they had the power to offend the religious beliefs of every sepoy in the army: covered with either pork or beef fat and with ends that had to be bitten off before they could be used, they were anathema to both Muslim and Hindu.

Thus the porcine origin of the cartridge lubricant became a major contributory factor in the Mutiny that began at Meerut (ironically the HQ of one of the leading pig-sticking clubs) on 10 May 1857, when soldiers imprisoned for refusing to touch the cartridges were rescued by others. In the bloody battles that followed, thousands of British and Indian soldiers and civilians were killed.

## Practical Pigs

The pig, if I am not mistaken,
Supplies us sausage, ham and bacon.
Let others say his heart is big –
I call it stupid of the pig.

*Ogden Nash* The Pig

Not only does the pig supply some fairly obvious edibles, it also provides almost 500 different products, giving weight to the saying that 'its squeal is the only thing that has no use'.

Pigskin is one of the most versatile of leathers since the presence of bristle follicles enables it to breathe better than most other animal skins.

Below its surface, the pig has also proved his value to man. Apart from the other primates (monkeys and apes), the pig is the creature physiologically most similar to us: its anatomical affinities include its omnivorous diet, with a digestive system remarkably like that of man, and distinctly comparable skin, blood and dentition. In consequence portions of a pig's heart are successfully used for making artificial heart valves for humans; its skin is employed as a temporary covering for burn patients, and so-called 'mini-pigs' bred to approximate human weight are used to test the effects of radiation and alcohol on a living body.

From the pig's generous body are extracted such human lifesavers as insulin for diabetics, heparin, an agent used as a blood anticoagulant in treating thrombosis, thyroxine for treating underactive thyroid glands and ACTH (adrenocorticotropic hormone), a pituitary gland extract for treating such disabilities as rheumatoid arthritis and rheumatic fever. Thank you, pigs!

*The thrill of the boar hunt depicted here in an original drawing by a master pig sticker of the Raj, Robert Baden-Powell.*

## SPORTING PIGS

### Boar Hunting

The speed and ferocity of the wild boar have made him one of man's most formidable adversaries since prehistoric times. The legendary boar hunts, that are so much a staple of European mythology, were paralleled in reality in ancient Greece and Rome, and throughout Europe until relatively modern times – and in certain areas, such as in parts of Germany and in Poland and New Zealand, continue today. Boar-hunting was one of the most dangerous sports of all time, resulting in the deaths of many hunters: Robert de Vere, 9th Earl of Oxford, was killed by a boar in 1395. The fearsome boar also became a synonym for savagery: one of the great tearaways of his day, Guillaume, Comte de la Marck, executed in 1485, was nicknamed 'The Wild Boar of the Ardennes'.

In *Venus & Adonis*, Shakespeare's

first published work, he describes something of the menacing power of the boar in Venus's warning to Adonis as she distracts him from the hunt:

'Thou hadst been gone,' quoth she,
 'sweet boy, ere this.
But that thou told'st me
 thou would hunt the boar.
O! be advis'd; thou know'st not
 what it is
With javelin's point a churlish
 swine to gore,
  Whose tushes never sheath'd he
   whetteth still
  Like to a mortal butcher,
   bent to kill.

On his bow-back he hath
 a battle set
Of bristly pikes, that ever
 threat his foes;
His eyes like glow-worms shine
 when he doth fret;
His snout digs sepulchres
 where'er he goes;

Being mov'd, he strikes
 what'er is in his way,
And whom he strikes his
 crooked tushes slay.'

And never was there truer advice:
Adonis is duly slain by a boar.

Hunting combined with the shrinking of Britain's forests contributed to the demise of the wild boar in Britain. In Shakespeare's day, the Earl of Essex killed the last boar in the county of Essex and in 1617 James I killed the last in the royal park at Windsor. In an attempt to restock the declining boar population Charles I obtained a breeding pair of boars from Germany and set them loose in the New Forest, but although they bred successfully, they were also hunted to extinction. It was not until the British Raj in India that the English gentleman could once again demonstrate his prowess as a boar hunter.

## Pig-sticking A Hundred Years Ago

India provided all the ingredients for exciting boar hunting or 'pig-sticking' – plenty of animals, native servants and a class with the leisure and military inclination to enjoy hunting.

The Meerut Tent Club was one of the foremost of India's many boar hunting clubs, the members of which were pukka sahibs to a man. Their meticulous log records every detail of every pig they ever stuck; the entry for 15 October 1885, for example, begins:

'Met at Jhureena. Spears, General Wilkinson, Clowes, Irwin, Mahon, Goulburn and Heygate. Four pig were reported by Lutchman [the club's native pig-spotter] to be living in rideable jungle so we went out to look for them. First beat along the side of the Burha Gunga opposite Jhureena, but saw nothing except a blue bull. Wheeling to the right into the maiden, a big sow and several young ones got up and when we got into the jheel near the hills a small boar broke loose, closely followed by Clowes, Mahon, Irwin and the General. The General unfortunately had a fall in a boggy part of the jheel but was not hurt. Clowes obtained the spear just as piggy reached firm ground and then his horse also slipped up and fell. But the pig was soon despatched by the remainder.'

The Club log records that in 1885–86 season, 85 boar were killed.

British officers such as Robert Baden-Powell, founder of the Boy Scout movement, achieved fame as champion pig-stickers. For many the sport became an obsession: the appendix to *Modern Pig Sticking* (1914) contains a selection of 'Indian Pig-sticking Songs', including *The Boar*, sung to tune of *My Love is Like the Red, Red Rose*. On the right is one verse of it.

---

The boar, the mighty boar's
    my theme,
Whate'er the wise may say,
My morning though, my midnight
    dream,
My hope throughout the day.

---

Youth's daring spirit, manhood's
    fire,
Firm hand and eagle eye,
Must they acquire who do aspire
To see the grey boar die.

---

Then pledge the boar, the mighty
    boar
Fill high the cup with me;
Here's a health to all who fear no
    fall,
And the next grey boar we see!

---

### 'Swine Harry'

In his *Table Book* (1827–28) William Hone tells of 'a field on the side of Pinnow, a hill in Lothersdale in Craven', known as 'Swine Harry'. Its strange name is said to derive from that of a pig thief who led a stolen pig by night on the end of a rope; as he crossed a stile, to leave both hands free, he put the rope round his neck, but as he slipped the pig pulled tight, strangling him.

### Pig Transport

In Rome, the very nasty Emperor Heliogabalus had a chariot drawn by pigs. Pigs were also used as draught animals to pull ploughs in Minorca and parts of Scotland. In the early 19th century an eccentric farmer caused a stir in St Albans, Hertfordshire, when he galloped into the city in a cart drawn by four large pigs. He had spent six months training them. Even today, at country fairs authentic piggyback rides are given.

## Pig Criminals

In the Middle Ages, trials of animals were not uncommon in Europe. On 10 January 1457 in Savigny-sur-Étang in France a sow and six piglets were charged with murdering and partly eating a child. The sow was found guilty and sentenced to death, but the piglets were released on account of their youth, the bad example of their mother and since there was no evidence that they had taken part in eating the victim.

In 1846 at Pleternica, Slavonia, a pig that had allegedly devoured the ears of a small girl was sentenced to death. Its owner was declared responsible and compelled to compensate the child for her loss.

In recent times, a 'guard pig' used by a marijuana grower in Florida bit two sheriff's deputies before being taken into custody.

*The sow and piglets on trial for murder at Savigny-sur-Étang in 1457.*

## A Celebrated Gun-pig

In certain forests where dogs were prohibited, pigs were used as substitutes. At the beginning of the 19th century Sir Henry Mildmay owned a remarkable sow called Slut. Bred and trained in the New Forest, she learned '. . . to point and retrieve game as well as the best pointer.' Slut apparently had a sense of smell far superior to that of any hunting dog, and was highly regarded both for her abilities and for her enthusiasm.

*Sir Henry Mildmay's talented gun-pig, Slut, in retriever mode.*

## The Widow's Pig

Such was Dame Fripp, whom Mr Gilfil, riding leisurely in top-boots and spurs from doing duty at Knebley one warm Sunday afternoon, observed sitting in the dry ditch near her cottage, and by her side a large pig, who with that ease and confidence belonging to perfect friendship, was lying with his head in her lap and making no effort to play the agreeable beyond an occasional grunt.

'Why, Mrs Fripp?' said the Vicar, 'I didn't know you had such a fine pig. You'll have some rare flitches at Christmas!'

'Eh, God forbid! My son gev him me two 'ear ago, an' he's been company to me iver sin'. I couldn't find it i' my heart to part wi'm, if I niver knowed the taste o' bacon fat again.'

'Why, he'll eat his head off, and yours too. How can you go on keeping a pig and making nothing of him?'

'Oh, he picks a bit hisself wi' rooting, and I dooant mind doing wi'out to gi him summat. A bit o' company's meat an' drink too, an' he follers me about, and grunts when I spake to 'm, just like a Christian.'

*George Eliot* Scenes of Clerical Life, *1857*

## Truffle-hunting

Truffles are a fungus belonging to the Ascomycetes family much prized, particularly in France and Italy, for their culinary uses. Their principal disadvantage, though, is that they grow several inches below the ground and are thus extremely difficult to find – and consequently absurdly expensive. In the Perigord region of France the black Perigord truffle, *Tuber melanosporum*, is sought in winter months by *chercheuses*, pigs usually under five years of age with a far more acute sense of smell than that of any dog – their rivals in the pursuit of the elusive truffle. Some champion truffle-hunters are reputed to be able to sniff one out from 6 metres/20 feet away (an ability that has also been

*(Above) A typical Périgord truffle-hunting pig, with its typical Toulouse-Lautrec lookalike master. (Left) Being worth its weight in gold, the truffle – and its seeker – is a fitting subject for jewellery.*

used to great effect by police with pigs trained to sniff out drugs). The major disadvantage of using pigs, though, is that they adore truffles and their owners often have to do battle with them for the prize.

## Famous Porcinophiles

Not all friendships with pigs have been forged by rustic pig-keepers. In fact, there seems to have been a tradition of amity between the British aristocracy and their pigs: 'Peter Pindar' (the satirical poet John Wolcot, 1738–1819) wrote a stanza on the death of Lady Mount Edgecumbe's favourite pig, 'Cupid', and in 1665 an Ethiopian hog was sent as a well-received gift to the Prince of Orange. The eminent politician, Lord Hartington (Spencer Cavendish, 1833–1908), a close friend of King Edward VII, was in the House of Lords one day when he heard a fellow peer remark of some event, 'This is the proudest moment of my

life.' The Duke turned to his neighbour and murmured, 'The proudest moment of *my* life was when my pig won the first prize at Skipton Fair!' His achievement was exceeded only in the pages of fiction when Lord Emsworth's pig, Empress of Blandings, in P. G. Wodehouse's Blandings books, won first prize in the Shropshire County Agricultural Show's fat pig class *three* times running. Other notable pig owners have included Sir Walter Scott, Archbishops of Canterbury from Thomas à Becket to Robert Runcie, singer James Taylor and publisher and novelist Michael Korda. James Dean was also a great porcinophile, having been brought up on a farm. There is a well known photograph of him with a fat pig rubbing against his leg.

*'A cat may look at a king' – and so may a pig: visiting a farm in 1942, George VI notes that pigs are pulling their weight in the war effort.*

## Piggy Prizes

'Bowling for a pig' – a bowling contest in which the prize is a piglet – and catching greased or soaped pigs, sometimes known as 'pig-running', have long been popular sideshows at country fairs. In Poet Laureate Ted Hughes' poem, *View of a Pig*, he describes a greased piglet he chased at a fair that was 'faster and nimbler than a cat'. Pig racing is popular in Iowa and other pig-rearing parts of America, where 'pig clubs' were, particularly in the 1920s, as popular among teenagers as discos are today, and where 'swine judging' has been raised to the status of a fine art.

## The Dunmow Flitch

By ancient tradition if a person going to Dunmow in rural Essex on Whit Monday could, while enduring kneeling on two sharp stones at the church door, swear he (or – but only in modern times – she) had been married happily for the past 12 months and a day, had never argued or wished to have been unmarried, they could win a prize of a 'flitch' or side of bacon. Little is known of the origins of this strange custom – which is believed to be similar to those once observed in Whichenowe, Staffordshire and St Meleine, Brittany. It is said to have been started by an aristocratic lady, Juga, in 1111 and to have been restored by Robert de Fitzwalter in 1244. The names of several flitch-winners from the medieval period are recorded. The custom was even alluded to in Chaucer's tale of *The Wife of Bath*. It was frequently dropped and revived – and the revival in the 19th century was due to the novelist Harrison Ainsworth who in 1855 acted as the judge who cross-examined the claimants.

## 'The Hog-faced Gentlewoman'

In an age when prodigies of all kinds offered the sensations that tabloid newspapers provide today, the case of the 'Hog-faced Gentlewoman' captured the public's imagination. In a pamphlet dated 1640, the anonymous author related the story of 'Mistris Tannakin Skinker', who was said to have been born in 'Wirkham', Holland, in 1618, '. . . all the limbes and lineaments of her body well featur'd and proportioned, only her face, which is the ornament and beauty of the rest, had the Nose of a Hog, or Swine, which was not only a stain and blemish, but a deformed uglinesse, making all the rest loathsome, contemptible and odious to all that look upon her'.

The cause of this tragic phenomenon was, of course, put down to witchcraft: her mother, while pregnant with Tannakin, was said to have been offhand with a witch who begged

*Mistris Tannakin Skinker, 'The Hog-faced Gentlewoman', responds to a greeting with her customary grunt.*

for money, and in consequence the witch was heard to swear, 'As the Mother is Hoggish, so Swinish shall be the Child'. A local magician called Vandermast was called in and advised that if she succeeded in marrying a gentleman, the spell would be broken and her hog-face replaced by a conventional visage. By covering her head with a black bag – and offering the inducement of a £40,000 dowry – Tannakin's parents lured many suitors, but none could go through with the challenge: a Scotsman rushed away declaring '. . . hee could endure no Porke'. The story has no satisfactory ending: it is hinted that 'Mistris Tannakin' eventually settled in London and lived in great luxury – but as a hog-faced spinster.

## 'The Pig-faced Lady of Manchester Square'

All London thrilled to the revelation, early in 1815, that there was living in fashionable Manchester Square a woman of Irish ancestry, 'well-born', but with something of a social problem. Aged about twenty, wealthy and with a beautiful body, she might well have attracted droves of fortune-hunters, but for the fact that her beautiful body was surmounted by a pig's head. Like Tannakin Skinker before her, she was said to eat, pig-like, from a silver trough, and to communicate by grunting. Her female attendant, although paid the then huge salary of £1,000 a year, quit in fright, and as a result *The Times* of 9 February carried an advertisement for a replacement. A week later, *The Morning Herald* contained an advertisement from a gentleman offering to marry her if he could be formally introduced to her. In a broadsheet an artist called 'Fairburn (Senior)'

*The Pig-Faced Lady of Manchester Square, in fashionable Regency attire, presiding over her* salon. *After Caroline Lamb, Charlotte Pig?*

provided a good portrait of this monstrosity, but a subsequent rival broadsheet containing a sketch by 'a medical gentleman who constantly attends her' refuted both that she lived in Manchester Square and that she had received offers of marriage. The veracity of either version was called into question when an almost identical story was reported from Dublin at about the same time.

## Pigs On The Stage

At the turn of the century, Edward S. Holder of Indiana, toured the music halls of America and Europe with his troupe of ten black hogs. Said to be the largest number of performing pigs ever trained, they pulled a cart with a dog 'driver', stormed a fortress held by pig soldiers, walked a tightrope, balanced on a see-saw and on barrels and played musical instruments. Holder was not alone as a presenter of stage-struck piggies – as recently as the late 1950s, Sanger's Circus had Bill, a performing pig.

## The Texas 'Swine Dive'

The modern equivalent of the performing hogs of yesteryear can be found at the Aquarena Springs, San Marcos, Texas. Known as the 'Swine Dive', it is a sort of dolphinarium, but featuring aquatic pigs. Here four trained animals, all confusingly – or simply – called 'Ralph', under the watchful eye of trainer Sonny Marston, perform for nearly a million visitors a year – attracted perhaps by a striking roadside sign depicting a pig in scuba diving equipment with the slogan, 'Have you ever seen a pig swim?' If nothing else, the diving pigs (lured into the pool by babies' bottles filled with milk), refute the folk belief that when pigs take to water they cut their own throats with their trotters.

## Louis XI's Musical Pigs

The Abbot of Baigne, a man of great wit, and who had the art of inventing new musical instruments, being in the service of Louis XI, king of France, was ordered by that prince to get him a concert of swine's voices, thinking it impossible. The abbot was not surprised, but asked money for the performance, which was immediately delivered him; and he wrought a thing as singular as ever was seen. For out of a great number of hogs, of several ages, which he got together, and placed under a tent or pavilion, covered with velvet, before which he had a table of wood, painted, with a certain number of hogs, he made an organical instrument, and as he played upon the said keys, with little spikes which pricked the hogs he made them cry in such order and consonance, as highly delighted the king and all his company.

*Nathaniel Wanley*
Wonders of the Little World, *1678*

This original, if cruel, music-maker was more or less copied by the inventor of the so-called 'Porco-Forte', described in 1839, an instrument that was said to have been invented in Cincinnati whereby pigs' tails were pinched in order to produce a range of squealed notes.

### 'Learned Pigs'

It took the 'Age of Reason' to come up with something as unreasonable as the 'Learned Pig'. At the end of the 18th century, by way of contradicting the rationalists of the day, there was a flurry of piggy performers, one of the first of which was exhibited at Nottingham in 1784 and described to Dr Samuel Johnson, eliciting the comment, '. . . pigs are a race unjustly calumniated!' – though some, less convinced, and declaring that these talented pigs were actually agents of the devil, urged that they should be burnt at the stake.

In his *Diary of a Country Parson* for 19 December 1785 the Revd James Woodforde recorded his visit to Norwich where he paid a shilling to see a 'learned Pigg':

After Dinner the Captain and myself went and saw the learned Pigg . . . It was wonderful to see the sagacity of the Animal! It was a Boar Pigg, very thin, quite black and with a magic Collar on his Neck. He would spell any word or Numbers from the Letters and Figures that were placed before him.

A 'learned pig' advertised in *The Daily Universal Register* (afterwards *The Times*) in 1785 'casts accounts', could tell the time, distinguish colours and read ladies' (but apparently not men's) thoughts. The species was apparently sufficiently common for William Wordsworth to include a reference to one in *The Prelude* in his description of St Bartholomew Fair.

One of the most celebrated was 'Toby, the Sapient Pig' who '. . . will

*Toby brushes up on the classics and pens a novel before feeding time.*

spell and read; cast accounts; play at cards; tell any person what o'clock it is to a minute . . . and discover a person's thoughts . . . must be seen to be believed'. Toby was exhibited in London in 1817 and immortalized in Thomas Hood's poem, *The Lament of Toby*, in *The Comic Annual* for 1835, from which the following is a short extract (it is a *very* long poem!):

> Of what avail that I could spell
>     And read just like my betters,
> If I must come to this at last,
>     To litters, not to letters?
>
> O, why are pigs made scholars of?
>     It baffles my discerning,
> What griskins, fry and chitterlings
>     Can have to do with learning.
>
> Alas! my learning once drew cash,
>     But public fame's unstable,
> So I must turn a pig again,
>     And fatten for the table.

# PIGS MIGHT FLY

## The Pig In Mythology And Folklore

I N ANCIENT EGYPT PIGS WERE believed to be unclean and unlucky. They were dedicated to the evil god Set, and the souls of evil people were said to inhabit pigs. Even touching one was taboo – anyone who did so was obliged to leap into the Nile fully clothed to purify himself. Swineherds were thought of as 'untouchables' and were forbidden to enter temples or to marry outside their group. (Similar beliefs were held elsewhere in the ancient Middle East, hence when in the Bible the Prodigal Son is reduced to serving as a swineherd it is seen as an ultimate degradation.) The only exception to the taboo was when the pig was sacrificed in midwinter to the Moon or to the god Osiris, after which it could be eaten safely.

Sacrifices of pigs and boars were highly regarded in ancient Greece. In *The Iliad*, Agamemnon sacrifices a boar to Zeus and Helios; pigs were sacrificed to Demeter, the goddess of agriculture because in a confused legend they either ravaged her crops or helped her by turning the earth with their snouts. One version tells of how Demeter's swineherd Eubuleus was a witness to the rape of Demeter's daughter Persephone by Hades, when the ground swallowed up her and his pigs. At the Thesmophoria Festival at Eleusis, the homeland of Eubuleus, live pigs were hurled off a cliff in his honour. Their remains were used to fertilise seed the next year to ensure a plentiful harvest.

The Cretans worshipped pigs and believed that the god Zeus was suckled by a sow and that a squealing pig drowned the cries of baby Zeus and thereby saved him from being eaten by Cronos. In ancient Crete, pigs

*The return of the Prodigal Son – his lowly status is symbolized by his occupation as a swineherd.*

were sacrificed to Ceres at the beginning of the harvest and to Bacchus at the beginning of the vintage.

No animal was more popular than the pig as a sacrifice in sealing Roman treaties. Representatives of both parties would go to the Temple of Jupiter where the priest would slaughter it with the words, 'If the Roman people injure this pact, may Jupiter smite them, as I smite this pig with the stone', whereupon he smashed a rock down upon the victim's skull.

### Unclean: Pig Taboos

And the swine, though he divide the hoof, and be cloven-footed, yet he cheweth not the cud; he is unclean to you.

*Leviticus xi.7*

The Jews, Syrians, Arabs, Ethiopian Coptic Christians, Mandaeans and certain other Middle Eastern peoples forbade the eating of pork. There is much argument about the origin of this taboo. Tacitus, the Roman historian, declared that Israelites did not eat pork because they caught a kind of 'leprosy' from it. In the *Golden Bough* Sir James Frazer suggested their avoidance resulted from their holding the pig to be so sacred that they could not bring themselves to injure it. The truth is probably more mundane: pigs are notoriously difficult to care for among nomads, compared with grazing animals such as sheep. It therefore seems highly likely that nomadic peoples, considering themselves superior to and being prejudiced against the food customs of their enemies or conquered peoples, rejected the pig of the settled tribes of the Middle East. The supposed connection with the climate and alleged unhygienic nature of pork is untenable, as it is eaten without ill effects in hot countries of South East Asia and in New Guinea.

The Jewish prohibition on eating pork led in the Middle Ages to the appearance of the anti-Jewish motif of the 'Judensau', an obscene image of a Jew suckling a pig. During the Spanish Inquisition any obvious distaste for pork was seen to be heretical – and people went to the opposite extreme in an attempt to prove their faith, to the point where King Philip II of Spain made himself ill by gorging himself on bacon. Less familiar is the Scottish taboo on pork: many Scots believed that the pig was the devil incarnate and would not keep or eat them, so that when Dr Johnson toured the Highlands in 1773 he saw only one pig, in the Hebrides.

## GREAT BOARS OF MYTHOLOGY

### Ulysses' Companions

In *The Odyssey* Ulysses' companions were turned into swine by the sorceress Circe on her island of Aeaea. Ulysses himself escaped, and later

*Circe the enchantress turns Ulysses' men into swine. By Victorian artist Briton Rivière (1840–1920).*

succeeded in having the spell reversed. Aeaea was said in reality to be Circeii on the coast of Italy – and on Monte Circeo wild pigs and boars are still described to visitors as 'Ulysses' Companions'.

## Proteus

In *The Odyssey*, King Agamemnon's brother, Menelaus, pursues the Egyptian god Proteus, who changes into various animals, including a gigantic wild boar. Proteus' ability to change shape (from which the word 'protean' is derived) is similar to that of the 'Baldanders' in Grimmelshausen's *The Adventuresome Simplicissimus* (1669), which turns itself into two piggy incarnations – a fat sow – and a sausage – as well as a field of clover and a pile of manure.

## The Erymanthian Boar

The Erymanthian Boar was a gigantic beast living in the cypress groves of Mount Erymanthius and on Mount

*Hercules captures the Erymanthian Boar and crams it into a storage jar.*

Lampeia, from which it terrorized the neighbouring region. Hercules set out as his fourth labour to capture it alive. He shoved it in a snow drift, bound it with chains and carried it to Mycenae. Its tusks were said to have been exhibited in the Temple of Apollo at Cumae. Some authorities have viewed the Egyptian acceptance of pork only in midwinter, and the Yuletide boar's head of Northern European tradition as relating to this legend.

## The Calydonian Boar

When Oeneus, King of Calydon in Aetolia, failed to make suitable sacrifices to the goddess Artemis, she sent the Calydonian Boar (said to be the offspring of Phaea) to ravage his lands. A group of heroes, including Jason, Theseus, Castor, and Atalanta hunted it. After killing a number of the hunters it was slain by the King's supposed son Meleager. According to the Greek travel writer Pausanius,

tusks three feet long were exhibited at Tegea as those of the Calydonian Boar.

## The Boar's Revenge

The mythological boar hunts were not all one-sided: in certain versions of ancient legends, Tammuz, Ancaeus, Zeus (in Cretan legend only), Carmanor of Lydia, Attis (in the Lydian version only) and Adonis were among many gods and heroes slain by boars; boar disguise was also fashionable for killers, including Set when he killed Osiris.

Adonis had been born when a boar ripped open a tree, and was later slain in a forest by a boar; from his blood sprang the anemone. Adonis was also the name given to the sacred boar that was hunted and killed annually but reborn afterwards – a legend perpetuated under different names in Viking tradition.

## Celtic Pig-Lore

Numerous Celtic legends involve pigs: the Celtic Earth Mother, the Cailleach, had a pig attendant which was thought of as a devil; Celtic warriors were buried with boar tusks; the Celtic afterworld, like that of the Vikings, offered an inexhaustible supply of pork, the meat most highly esteemed in the Celtic world: Manannan's pigs, though killed and eaten, were alive and ready to eat again the next day.

In *The Mabinogion*, a collection of Celtic stories, there is an Arthurian hero called Kilhwch whose name means literally 'pig sty'. *The Mabinogion* also describes the hunting of Twrch Trwyth, a powerful boar with seven offspring: King Arthur and his knights hunt them to Ireland in an attempt to secure the magic comb, razor and shears kept between its ears.

A Welsh myth relates the story of an Old White Sow, Hen Wen, who is tended by a magician/swineherd, Coll ap Collfrewr. In Welsh folklore, there are pig apparitions on Halloween, and during eclipses people are said to grunt like pigs. It was also thought that St Elmo's fire (atmospheric electrical discharges) could be dispersed by the squeal of a pig.

## The Everlasting Viking Boar

The Vikings believed that slain warriors gathered for a great feast in the hall of Valhalla where the god Odin's cook, Abdhrimnir, prepared a feast of pork from the magic boar, Sehrimner, in his huge cauldron, Eldhrimnir. The extraordinary feature of the meal was that however many warriors feasted, and however many slices they carved from Sehrimner, the next day he was as good as new and the feast could begin again.

## Yeats And The Black Pig

Celtic mythology and Irish folklore dwell at length on pigs of all sorts – in fact, one of the ancient names of Ireland was *Muic-inis*, or 'pig island'. According to one legend, Fin mac Cool slew Diarmuid when he was disguised as a boar. It was believed that illnesses could be cured by walking three times round a pig sty and that a pig driven into a house on May morning was lucky, but unlucky during the rest of the year. The poet W. B. Yeats (1865–1939), fascinated by these legends, wrote 'Swine of the Gods' in his *The Celtic Twilight* (1893). He also discovered the myth of a black pig known as the 'croppy black sow'. It was viewed as an apocalyptic beast that appears in the legend of 'Valley of the Black Pig' (which Yeats used as the title of one of his poems in *The Wind Among the Reeds*, 1899), a place where the enemies of Ireland would be defeated. Apparitions of black pigs were there-

fore seen as portents of troubles in Ireland, alongside the superstition of evil spirit in black pigs. So obsessed did Yeats become with black pigs that he was caricatured riding one.

## Ghostly Pigs

Danish pig-lore contains many descriptions of pig ghosts, especially headless sows, and tales of phantom sows running through villages with victims on their backs. In Zealand, there is a story of the 'Glum Sow' that rushes out at night scaring horses by kicking up sparks in the road with its tusks and which was blamed for all night driving accidents. In Britain, pig ghosts have been reported in Andover, Hampshire, and fairy pigs on the Isle of Man.

## The Boar That Saved The World

In Indian mythology, the third avatar (earthly incarnation) of Vishnu is in the form of a gigantic boar. According to the myth, the earth was submerged by an ocean demon, Hiranyaksha. A 1000-year battle ensued at the end of which Varaha, the boar, dived down to the bottom of the ocean and surfaced with the earth intact. In Indian art, Varaha is sometimes depicted as completely animal in form, sometimes just boar-headed. Earthquakes are said to be caused by Varaha shifting the weight of the earth from one tusk to the other.

## Good Companions

Homer regarded swineherds as 'divine', and associations between them and pigs, both tame and wild, persist in Christian legends. There are several ancient Irish myths in which boars care for a holy man's pigs, lick his wounded feet or entertain

*Vishnu as Varaha skilfully balances the rescued world on his tusks.*

him by making music; but the most prevalent stories link pigs with saints:

### St Anthony And The 'Tantony Pig'

St Anthony is universally known as the patron of hogs.

*Thomas Fuller* Worthies of England, *1662*

St Anthony is the patron saint of swineherds. Pigs were originally associated with him as symbols of the vices and the temptations to which he was exposed, but later many legends arose linking him with pigs: he was asked to heal the son of the King of the Lombards in Italy, but chose to heal a lame, blind piglet first.

John Stow in his *Survey of London* (1598) explained that pigs that were deemed unsuitable for sale were let loose with bells round their necks supplied by the Proctor of St Anthony's Hospital in London (founded in 1242 and destroyed in 1666 in the Great Fire). The St Anthony or 'tantony'

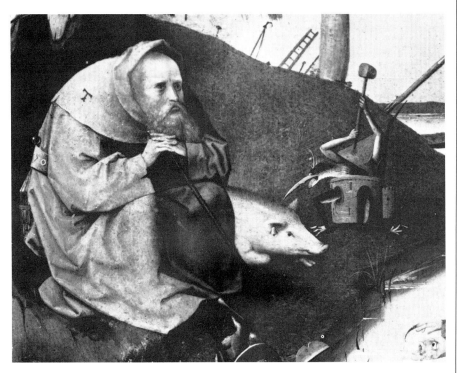

*St Anthony and a 'tantony pig' with a bell, by Hieronymus Bosch,* c. 1490.

pigs were allowed to scavenge and used for the benefit of patients in the hospital, whom they supplied with meat and the lard used in treating skin disease; they followed blindly anyone who fed them, so the term 'tantony pig' became used for anyone who did the same.

### St Brannoc

At the church of St Brannoc, Braunton, Devon, a carving depicts the sow and piglets which led St Brannoc to the site of the church where he is buried.

### St Malo

This 7th century missionary monk in Brittany, after whom the port of St Malo is named, came upon a weeping swineherd who, in attempting to prevent a sow from destroying corn, had hurled a stone at it and accidentally killed it, leaving seven orphaned piglets and a potentially enraged master. St Malo prayed and laid his

staff on the dead sow's ear, reviving it. When the swineherd told his master, he gave a field to St Malo's church.

### St Oswald

St Oswald's Church, Winwick, Lancashire, has a carving of a pig on its west front commemorating the pig that demolished the newly-built portions of the church every day and carried the rubble to a nearby spot where St Oswald died and where the church was ultimately built.

### St Kentigern

St Asaph's Cathedral, North Wales, was founded by St Kentigern on ground that was thoughtfully tilled by a wild boar.

## PIG SUPERSTITIONS

### Doctor Pig

The pig has been regarded as a source of all manner of preventative and curative medicines since early times. Boars' tusks were once widely used as protective amulets. Infusions brewed from them were used to cure epilepsy and toothache. An Irish tale tells of the skin of a magic pig that heals with just a touch; in Denmark smoked pork rind was used to get rid of warts by being rubbed on them and then buried in a place where no-one walked, while in Poland piggy potions cured epilepsy, and in the Aegean islands, incontinence. Antonine monks in the Middle Ages bred pigs for their lard which was used as a supposed cure for 'St Anthony's fire' (ergotism or erysipelas, a skin disease).

### King's Evil

The disease known as 'scrofula' was so-called from the Latin, *scrofulae*, which means 'little sows' – sows being thought to be vulnerable to tuberculosis of the lymph glands. Scrofula was also called the 'king's evil' because it was once believed that the touch of a king could cure sufferers. Touching was introduced in England in the Middle Ages, reaching a peak under Charles II who was alleged to have touched 100,000 victims.

### Don't Say A Word...

The belief that pigs could 'see the wind' and that they are agents of the devil led to their being feared by fishermen. Even the word, 'pig' was banned at sea, and alternative words, such as 'grumphie', 'curlie-tail', 'guffey', 'the Grecian' and 'the article' were used instead. The potentially awful effects of inadvertently using the prohibited word could be counteracted by touching a ringbolt and saying 'cold iron', or by holding up thumbs and crossing forefingers. One might pause to wonder, however, how often the average fisherman actually *needs* to use the word 'pig' at sea...

This strange belief may relate to the association between the pig and the 'devil's mark' – marks on pigs' trotters where the devil was believed to have entered the Gadarene swine; at one time, even people safely on dry land would mutter 'cold iron' and touch the nails on their boots when they heard the story of the Gadarene swine in church. It may also be connected with the belief that pigs 'see the wind', which is more significant to sailors than anyone else – in Scotland and north-east England, especially among fishermen, the word 'pig' was avoided by saying 'the short-legged', 'the grunting one', or even 'the beautiful one', and there are families in which it is regarded as unlucky to say the word 'pig'; nor was this superstition confined to Europe: in China the euphemism, 'the long-nosed general', is sometimes used instead of the dreaded 'pig'.

## OTHER PIG SUPERSTITIONS

◆

### Denmark

Sows were serviced just before full moon: the greater the number of days after the new moon, the greater the litter.

The sow was then given barley: the number of handfuls would equal the number of piglets (perhaps prompting the temptation to force-feed the pig).

On servicing day, the pig farmer would cut a notch at the base of his thumbnail; when this had grown out, the sow would be ready to farrow.

Piglets were held over a smoking fire to make them thrive and to ward off curses.

It was thought to be bad luck to hit a pig with a broom: it hindered its putting on weight and gave it worms.

### Germany

A folklorist of 1870 writing in *Notes & Queries* recorded some strange pig superstitions that were then current in Mecklenburg:

A blackthorn stick was placed in the left corner of pig sty to ward off witches.

Pigs were rubbed with dill seed to protect against the evil eye.

A sick pig was washed on three successive Fridays and fumed with burnt bark of cascarilla.

Pigsty wood was painted with special anti-witch paint, originating in Russia.

A horse's head was buried under the pig's trough to make it feed voraciously – though few pigs need any encouragement.

## A Porkpourri Of Weird Beliefs

The belief that pigs are immune to snake bites is not true – but their thick layer of fat may mean that venom is dispersed slowly, and hence not fatal. Indeed, some pigs are known to have gobbled poisonous snakes with relish.

The pig that suckles in front is believed to be strongest of the litter.

Pigs should not be killed when the moon is waning: their meat will shrink when it is being cooked.

Zulu girls believe that eating pork makes their children ugly.

Dragging a pig's tail across the ground makes it fertile.

Rowan hung round pigs' necks makes them fatten quickly.

The bite of a pig causes cancer.

Eating pig's brains makes the eater tell the truth.

## The Proverbial Pig

The popularity of pigs as domesticated animals has led to their being featured in a large number of proverbs. Some, such as 'Do not cast pearls before swine', have a biblical origin; the full version is: 'Give not that which is holy unto the dogs, neither cast ye your pearls before swine, lest they trample them under their feet and turn again and rend you.' (Matthew vii.6). And along similar lines: 'As a jewel of gold in a swine's snout, so is a fair woman which is without discretion' (Proverbs xi.22). 'Never buy a pig in a poke' is a common proverb that derives from the practice of dishonest traders who would sometimes substitute a cat in a 'poke' or bag for the pig a farmer had bought; to mix sayings, 'letting the cat out of the bag' would expose the deception.

## Some Piggy Proverbs

As good to the purse is a sow as a cow.

Better my hog dirty home than no hog at all.

A collier's cow and an alewife's sow are always well fed.

Draff [grain husks left over during brewing] is good enough for swine.

He has brought his pigs to a fine market.

He that can rear up a pig in his house Hath cheaper his bacon and sweeter his souse [salted meat].

He that hath one hog makes him fat; and he that hath one son makes him a fool.

A hog that's bemired tends to bemire others.

The hog never looks up to him that threshes down the acorns.

If you would live well for a week, kill a hog; if you would live well for a month, marry; if you would live well all your life, turn priest.

It is ill to drive black hogs in the dark.

Lead a pig to the Rhine, it remains a pig.

Little knoweth the fat sow what the lean doth mean.

He loves bacon well that licks the swinesty door.

You can not make a silk purse out of a sow's ear.

The young pig grunts like the old sow.

Sus Minervam docet, (a Latin proverb meaning a pig teaching Minerva – equivalent to 'teaching your grandmother to suck eggs').

A swine over fat is the cause of his own bane.

Swine, women and bees cannot be turned.

Unless your bacon you would mar Kill not your pig without the R (do not slaughter pigs in months without an 'R' in them, ie: during the summer).

What can you expect from a hog but a grunt?

You can pook and you can shove, but a Sussex pig he wun't be druv.

Pigs are either muck or money.

Pigs love that lie together.

Pigs may fly, but they are very unlikely birds.

Pigs might fly, if they had wings.

### Flying Pigs
The Paradise of my fancy is one where pigs have wings.
*G. K. Chesterton* Fancies Versus Fads, *1923*

'The time has come', the Walrus said,
  'To talk of many things:
Of shoes – of ships – and sealing wax –
  of cabbages – and kings –
And why the sea is boiling hot –
  And whether pigs have wings.'
*Lewis Carroll*
Through the Looking Glass, *1871*

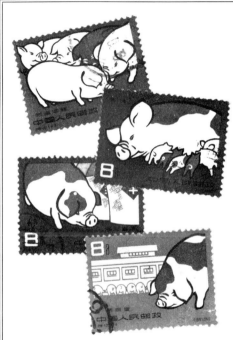

*Not only does the pig have a year named after it, but it is sufficiently revered by the Chinese to feature in a range of postage stamps.*

## The Chinese 'Year Of The Pig'

Buddha invited all the animals to come to him, but only twelve responded – the last, but not the least of these being the pig or wild boar. Buddha rewarded the loyal beasts by dedicating a year to each for ever more, and the year was to have its effect on those born in it, marking them with the animal's particular attributes and traits of character. People born in Chinese year of the pig are said to be honest, compassionate and courageous, lovers of beauty, freedom, nature and the outdoor life. 'Pig people' are frequently doctors or judges, poets and painters, foresters and philanthropists. Needless to remark, they love eating. Famous 'pigs' include Oliver Cromwell, Henry Ford, Henry VIII, Alfred Hitchcock and Ernest Hemingway.

The Chinese New Year, unlike the western, relates to the phases of the moon, and thus starts on a different date each year. First and last dates of pig years:

30 January 1911 – 17 February 1912
16 February 1923 – 4 February 1924
4 February 1935 – 23 February 1936
22 January 1947 – 9 February 1948
8 February 1959 – 27 January 1960
27 January 1971 – 14 February 1972
13 February 1983 – 1 February 1984
31 January 1995 – 18 February 1996

## PIG MONSTERS

The fertile imaginations of the compilers of bestiaries of mythological beasts have conjured up a veritable zoo of bizarre pig-like creatures:

### The Sea Hog

Described by John Swan in his *Speculum Mundi* (1635), it had a hog's head and the teeth and tusks of a boar – but a fishy tail and dragon's feet, One was found in the North Sea in 1537 and was reported to have been very fierce.

*Piggiwiggia Pyramidalis – Edward Lear's imaginative bacon plant.*

### The Ping-feng

This quite remarkable Chinese beast looks like a black pig – but has a head at each end.

### Piggiwiggia Pyramidalis

One of the least scary of all pig monsters, this exotic plant featuring piggy flowers was the creation of the master of nonsense, Edward Lear.

### The Catoblepas

Said by Pliny to inhabit the upper reaches of the Nile (Ethiopia), the Catoblepas was described by Gustave Flaubert in *The Temptation of St Anthony* as a '. . . black buffalo with the head of a pig'. If you so much as glimpse its eyes, you are struck dead on the spot.

### The 'Sow Harnessed With Chains'

The modern Argentinian monster *chancha con cadenas* or Tin Pig (*chancho de lata*) is said to make a frightful row as it clatters along railway tracks or even telegraph wires.

### A Toothy Piggy

Robert Burton in *Miracles of Art and Nature* (1678) describes '. . . hogs with Teeth growing out of their snouts, and as many behind their Ears'.

### 'The Wonderful Pig Of The Ocean'

A monster rejoicing in this spectacular name appears in the writings of the 16th century Swedish historian Olaus Magnus – who was not noted for his accuracy. This 'Monstrous Hog' was found in the German Ocean in 1537, '. . . it had a Hog's head, and a quarter of a Circle, like the Moon, in the hinde part of its head, four feet like a Dragon's, two eyes on both sides in his Loyns, and a third in his belly, inclined towards his Navel; behind he had a forked Tail, like to other Fish commonly.'

PLINY RECKONED HIS FELLOW Romans got through 20,000 pigs per annum, sent to their markets from Etruria, Gaul and Spain. Pig farming was developed into a major science and a detailed range of laws grew up relating to pig keeping, feeding, killing and the profession of pork butcher. Roman pigs were roasted whole or half roasted and half baked; hams were smoked and salted; sausages were made from chopped pork stuffed in intestines. Sows' wombs and udders were regarded as great delicacies, but were frowned upon by Pliny and other writers as outrageous extravagances. The Romans had many cruel ways of force feeding and killing pigs, which included a technique – not unlike that still used to produce *foie gras* in geese – by enlarging the liver of a sow by over feeding it with dried figs, mead and honeyed wine 'until they die with being overcharged'. The Greek writer

# FROM BOAR'S HEAD TO PETTITOE

## Pigs In The Kitchen

The pig,
by a merciful providence,
was given to mankind
solely for our benefit and
in order to supplement
our diet.
*Olaus Magnus (1490–1557)*

The hog is never good
but when he is in the dish.
*Popular saying*

Plutarch, who lived in Rome, complained of the Romans' use of a red hot poker thrust down the throats of pigs supposedly to improve the quality of the meat – a criticism echoed in Alexander Pope's attack on the 18th century English practice of whipping pigs to death to tenderize the meat: 'I know of nothing more shocking than the prospect of kitchens covered with blood and creatures expiring in torment.' Even in death the Roman passion for pig meat continued – hams were often buried in Roman tombs, with roast piglets reserved for the tombs of the wealthy.

**Fifty Fabulous Flavours**
No other animal can offer substance more fruitful to the talent of a cook. All other flesh has its own particular flavour; that of the pig presents us with a diversity of almost fifty flavours.
*Pliny* Natural History, *77* AD

## Going The Whole Hog

According to Pliny, 'The first Roman to serve up a whole boar at table was Servilus Rullus – a luxury which has today become a commonplace, for now we serve up at the table two or three boars at a time, and that not for the whole meal, but for the first course alone.' For sheer gluttony, though, the *Porcus Trojanus*, 'Trojan pig', would take some beating. Named in jocular reference to the capaciousness of the wooden horse of Troy, it was popular among upper class Romans and was the most elaborate of all pork dishes. It consisted of a whole pig stuffed with thrushes, larks, beccaficoes (small songbirds), oysters and nightingales, and was served in rich wine and gravy.

In *The Satyricon*, Petronius describes a banquet given by the wealthy Trimalchio: wild boar was served – with a cap on its head – on a huge dish, with baskets of dates dangling from its tusks and surrounded by

*A roast pig feast recalls the gastronomic excesses of ancient Rome, in Italian director Federico Fellini's boisterous film,* Roma *(1972).*

pastry piglets; when opened, a flock of thrushes flew out. Three white pigs were brought in, one selected and led away to be cooked. Another boar was produced, this time filled with sausages and blood puddings, followed by a goose surrounded by fish and game – all of which turn out to have been made of pork. And they call pigs greedy . . .

## Lamb On Pork

In 1828 the rather inappropriately-named Charles Lamb wrote *A Dissertation upon Roast Pork*. His ecstatic description is one of the most mouth-watering ever written.

'There is no flavour comparable, I will contend, to that of the crisp, tawny, well-watched, not over-roasted, crackling, as it is well called – the very teeth are invited to their share of the pleasure at this banquet in overcoming the coy, brittle resistance – with the adhesive oleaginous – O, call it not fat – but an indefinable

sweetness growing up to it – the tender blossoming of fat – fat cropped in the bud – taken in the shoot – in the first innocence – the cream and quintessence of the child-pig's yet pure food – the lean, not lean, but a kind of animal manna – or rather, fat and lean (if it must be so) so blended and running into each other, that both together make but one ambrosian result, or common substance.'

## The Origin Of Roast Pork

Charles Lamb also related a Chinese legend explaining the origin of roast pork: Bo-bo, the son of a swineherd, Ho-ti, was left in charge of his father's pigs and accidentally set fire to the family's house in which there just happened to be a pig. Contemplating his father's wrath, he dragged the immolated animal from the charred wreckage and then licked his fingers. He was amazed by the deliciousness of the flavour and managed to assuage Ho-ti's anger by introducing him to

his serendipitous culinary invention. The father and son team of Ho-ti and Bo-bo set up in business selling pork cooked by their closely guarded secret method – although burning down houses proved expensive until they hit upon the spit. The only question that remains unanswered is why did the Chinese invent swineherds before they knew how to cook a pig?

## 'Mountain Whale' On The Menu

In Japan, Buddhist meat-eating prohibitions led to the use of the term, 'mountain whale', as a euphemism for pork.

## The Kosher Pig?

It will come as a surprise to many to learn that some of the best pork in the world is produced – and indeed eaten – in Israel. Very much against the teachings of orthodox Judaism, pigs are reared not only in predominantly Christian Arab areas, such as

Nazareth, but also on several kibbutzim; it is obtainable in restaurants where it is often coyly described as 'white steak'. Now comes a further conundrum for rabbinical scholars: it has recently been suggested that a decidedly ugly wart-hog like creature known as the babirusa, a native of Indonesia, fulfils various criteria demanded of kosher animals, and for a time it looked as though 'kosher pork' might be available on Israeli menus; however, gourmets may wait in vain as there is considerable doubt about both the piggy attributes of the babirusa, and its commercial viability. They produce very small litters, have a long gestation period and are by no means as easily reared as the domesticated pig. Also, as the Indonesians have no qualms about eating them, they are nearly extinct.

*Before the kosher controversy: Thomas Bewick's woodcut of the babirusa.*

## Boar's Head

In Norse mythology, Freyr, god of peace and plenty, rode on the boar, Gullinbursti. At Yuletide, a boar was sacrificed in his honour – hence the old Christmas custom of serving a boar's head. 'A wylde bore's head gylt within a fayr platter' was served at the marriage feast of James IV of Scotland and Margaret in 1503 and when Prince Henry visited St John's College, Oxford, at Christmas in 1607, they served a boar's head and sung the 'Boar's Head Carol' which begins:

> The Boar is dead
> So, here is his head;
> What man could have done more
> Than his head off to strike,
> Meleager like
> And bring it as I do before?

In his *Sketch Book* (1820) the American writer Washington Irving, described the Christmas dinner he attended at Queen's College, Oxford where the 'Boar's Head Carol' was sung. This is a variant of an early 16th-century version which (with its Latin verses translated) goes as follows:

Bring back the boar's head,
Sounding praises to the Lord.

The bores hed in hondes I brings,
With garlondes gay and birdes
    singing:
I pray you all, help me to sing,
Who are at this banquet.

This boris hede I understond
Is cheff service in all this lond:
Wheresoever it may be fond
It is served with mustard.

The bores hede, I dare well say,
Anon, after the twelfth day,
He taketh his leve and goeth away,
Then he has left the country.

*Bringing in the boar's head, accompanied by the 'Boar's Head Carol' at Queen's College, Oxford, in 1846.*

## The 'Matanza'

The *matanza*, or pig slaughter, takes place in rural Spain in the winter, between November and February. Almost every part of the animal is made into some delicacy – hams, bacon, pork ribs, even the head, including the ears and feet, which are used in stews, prepared to a vast range of traditional recipes, including:

*Chicharones* – Crackling
*Chorizo* – Sausage
*Guena* – Inferior quality sausage
*Jamón serrano* – 'Mountain ham'
*Migas de matanza* – Breadcrumbs
    fried with lard and *torreznos*
    (lumps of bacon)
*Morcilla* – Blood sausage
*Tocino* – Salted back fat
*Torreznos* – Bacon slices

*Kitsch in the kitchen: a gourmet shrine dedicated to the pig, in just a few of its innumerable culinary and artistic manifestations.*

## Bacon On The Hoof

In 1870, as a publicity stunt, grocer Thomas Lipton had two gigantic pigs known as 'Lipton's Orphans' led through the streets of Glasgow bearing signs that read, 'I'm going to Lipton's, the best shop in town for Irish bacon'.

## Junk Food

The pig may provide us with a huge range of edible products; the one thing no self-respecting pig supplies, though, is the hamburger. Despite its name, they are supposed to be made from beef, and were originally called Hamburger Steaks after Hamburg in Germany where they originated. Names like 'Beefburger' and 'Eggburger' are therefore nonsensical: the only correct term for a hamburger-like object served in a bun can be an 'egg hamburger', or whatever.

Jambons.Saucissons.Salaisons.Conserves.

"ALHAMBRA"

*The pig as a motif of excellence in food and drink advertisements, with (left) a handy* aide-mémoire *for trainee pork butchers.*

*Pig butcher shop statuettes selling their brothers and sisters.*

## A Catalogue of Pig Dishes

The fifty flavours referred to by Pliny would today do scant justice to the international repertory of dishes that can be prepared from the pig. Here is just a taster:

**Bacon**

**Bath chaps** – The lower parts of the cheeks of a pig, cooked, but usually eaten cold

**Brains** – Eaten in places as far apart as France and Samoa

**Brawn** – Made from the pig's head or feet

**Cheeks**

**Hams** – British, including: York, Bradenham, Suffolk, Cumberland and Belfast; American, including: Kentucky and Virginia; European: including *jambon d'Ardennes*, *jambon de Bayonne* and *prosciutto de Parma*

**Hawaiian luau feasts** – At which a whole hog is cooked in an *imu*, or ground oven

**Papua New Guinea pigroast**

**Head cheese** – A kind of brawn made from pig or boar head

**Marzipan and sugar pigs** – Traditionally sold at fairs

**Pettitoes, or trotters**

**Pigs' ears and tails**

**Pig's fry**

**Pig's head**

**Pig's stomach** – 'Yrchins' and 'roasted hog's maw' are eaten by the Pennsylvania Dutch

**Pork pies** – Including Melton Mowbray pies, made from high quality local pigs

**Pork scratchings**

**Sausages** – From the German frankfurter and bratwurst to the Chinese *lop chong*

**Sucking pig** – Cooked in China, Spain, Germany, France and Russia to many different recipes

*Sides of bacon take pride of place in this meticulously detailed Victorian toy butcher's shop.*

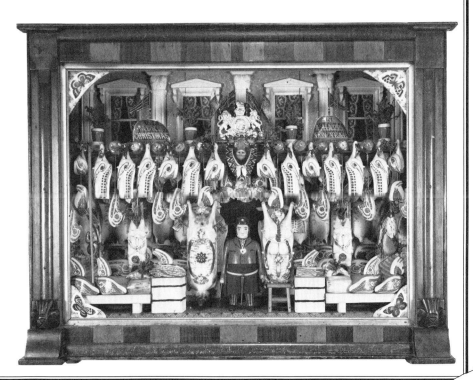

**S**INCE HOMER TOLD US OF Eumaios' love of pigs and described Circe's changing Odysseus' companions into pigs, the pig has featured in countless books. Epic boar hunts are found in Romance literature such as the *Song of Roland*, the Anglo-Norman *Boeve de Haumtone*, the *Romance of Sir Eglamour* and in the German *Niebelunglied*. More earthy pigs appear in Chaucer and provide moral guidance in the fables of Aesop and La Fontaine. Pigs make their presence felt in such novels as Henry Fielding's *The Adventures of Joseph Andrews*, which dwells on Parson Trulliber's love of pigs, in R. D. Blackmore's *Lorna Doone* and Thomas Hardy's *Jude the Obscure*. Napoleon, the pig, is the principal character in George Orwell's *Animal Farm* and pigs appear in William Golding's *Lord of the Flies*, in short stories such as Roald Dahl's *Pig* and in the James Herriot vet tales.

# PIGTALES

## The Literary Pig

*Pig bureaucrats get their snouts to the grindstone in the Walt Disney cartoon version of George Orwell's satirical novel,* Animal Farm (1945).

## Oedipus Tyrannus

*Oedipus Tyrannus; or, Swellfoot the Tyrant* is a satire with pig characters by Percy Bysshe Shelley. He wrote it in 1820 after he heard pigs being led to market when he was staying at Baths of San Giuliano in Italy. It satirically represents the matrimonial affairs of King George IV and Queen Caroline, with Lord Castlereagh and other British government ministers – accompanied by a chorus of pigs.

## Dreaming Pigs

Pigs grunt in a wet wallow-bath, and smile as they snort and dream. They dream of the acorned swill of the world, the rooting for pigfruit, the bag-pipe dugs of the mother sow, the squeal and snuffle of yesses of the women pigs in rut. They mud-bask and snout in the pig-loving sun; their tails curl; they rollick and slobber and snore to deep, smug, after-swill sleep.
*Dylan Thomas* Under Milk Wood, *1954*

## Empress of Blandings

Empress of Blandings appears in several novels by P. G. (known to his friends as 'Piggy'?) Wodehouse. She is the prize Berkshire belonging to Lord Emsworth who is first introduced in *Pig-hoo-o-o-o-ey!*, a short story in which she is off her food when the pig-man who looks after her is jailed. Lord Emsworth learns the secret of American hog-calling to which the Empress successfully responds. She goes on in other stories to be pignapped, threatened with dieting, running in the Grand National and joining Alcoholics Anonymous. She has a sequence of guardians including George Cyril Wellbeloved, Percy Pirbright, Edwin Pott and Monica Simmons, and we also meet Augustus Whiffle, (or Whipple), author of the definitive fictitious book on pigs, *The Care of the Pig* (Popgood & Grooly, 35 shillings) and encounter the piggy writings of Herr Wolff-Lehmann. Empress of Blandings,

*A 1935 collection of stories featuring Empress of Blandings, pig star of a galaxy of P. G. Wodehouse novels.*

whose two principal (and interrelated) roles in life are to make Lord Emsworth happy and to consume 57,800 calories of pigfood a day (however in *Galahad at Blandings* she was put on a diet and only had 5,700 calories a day), appears in *Summer Lightning* (1929), *Heavy Weather* (1933), *Full Moon* (1947), *Pigs Have Wings* (1952), *Service with a Smile* (1962) and *Galahad at Blandings* (1965).

## Hog-Calling

In *Pig-hoo-o-o-o-ey!*, the short story in which P. G. Wodehouse introduces us to Lord Emsworth's prize pig, Empress of Blandings, James Belford, suitor of his Lordship's niece, Angela, reveals the secrets of hog-calling learned in America:

'These calls vary in different parts of America. In Wisconsin, for example, the words *Poig, Poig, Poig* bring home – in both the literal and the figurative sense – the bacon. In

Illinois, I believe, they call *Burp, Burp, Burp*, while in Iowa the phrase *Kus, Kus, Kus* is preferred. Proceeding to Minnesota, we find *Peega, Peega, Peega* or, alternatively, *Oink, Oink, Oink*, whereas in Milwaukee, so largely inhabited by those of German descent, you will hear the good old Teuton *Komm Schweine, Komm Schweine*. Oh, yes, there are all sorts of pig calls, from the Massachusetts *Phew, Phew, Phew* to the *Loo-ey, Loo-ey, Loo-ey* of Ohio, not counting various local devices such as beating on tin cans with axes or rattling pebbles in a suit-case. I knew a man out in Nebraska who used to call his pigs by tapping on the edge of the trough with his wooden leg . . . but wait. I haven't told you all. There is a master word.'

'A what?'

'Most people don't know it, but I had it straight from the lips of Fred Patzel, the hog-calling champion of the Western states. What a man! I've known him to bring pork chops leaping from their plates. He informed me that, no matter whether an animal has been trained to answer to the Illinois *Burp* or the Minnesota *Oink*, it will always give immediate service in response to this magic combination of syllables. It is to the pig world what the Masonic grip is to the human. *Oink* in Illinois or *Burp* in Minnesota, and the animal merely raises its eyebrows and stares coldly. But go to either State and call *Pig-hoo-o-o-o-ey!* . . .'

## A Shocking Accident

Graham Greene's short story of this name recounts the effects of a bizarre accident: nine year-old Jerome is told of the death of his father, killed when a fifth-floor balcony in Naples collapses under the weight of the apartment's unlikely inhabitant – a pig. Inevitably, people treat the tragedy with ambivalence – it is indeed the 'shocking accident' of the title, but all who hear Jerome's account are irresistibly amused by its bizarre nature. After inventing versions of the story that will be thought less mirth-inducing, his fiancée is eventually told it quite bluntly by an aunt. He realises he loves her when she shares the reaction he had as a child – initial shock followed by the only possible question, 'What happened to the pig?'

## Pigs In Children's Books

Pigs feature as heroes in numerous nursery rhymes and children's books – further proof of the great affection in which they are held. Hans Christian Andersen, being Danish, could scarcely avoid writing about pigs: his *The Piggy Bank* was published in 1855. Many illustrators of juvenile literature included pigs, such as Henry Holiday whose illustrations for Lewis Carroll's *The Hunting of the Snark* (1876) include a pig band. The Victorian illustrator Walter Crane

*Henry Holiday's pig band in Lewis Carroll's* Hunting of the Snark.

devoted his talents to *This Little Pig His Picture Book* (1895), while Lewis Baumer's *Did You Ever* (1903) contains imaginative pictures of a pig orchestra, a pig artist and a pig policeman – attempting to stop a couple of road hogs. In recent years Helen Oxenbury's *Pig Tale* (1973) and books illustrated by Mary Rayner have maintained the nursery pig story tradition.

## Pig Baby

The baby grunted again, and Alice looked very anxiously into its face to see what was the matter with it. There could be no doubt that it had a *very* turn-up nose, much more like a snout than a real nose: also its eyes were getting extremely small for a baby: altogether Alice did not like the look of the thing at all.

'But perhaps it was only sobbing,' she thought, and looked into its eyes again, to see if there were any tears.

No, there were no tears. 'If you're going to turn into a pig, my dear,' said Alice, seriously, 'I'll have nothing more to do with you. Mind now!' The poor little thing sobbed again, (or grunted, it was impossible to say which), and they went on for some time in silence.

Alice was just beginning to think to herself, 'Now, what am I going to do with this creature, when I get it home?' when it grunted again, so violently, that she looked down into its face with some alarm. This time there could be *no* mistake about it: it was neither more nor less than a pig, and she felt that it would be quite absurd for her to carry it any further.

'By-the-bye, what became of the baby?' said the Cat, 'I'd nearly forgotten to ask.'

'It turned into a pig,' Alice answered very quietly . . .

'I thought it would,' said the Cat, and vanished again.

*Lewis Carroll* Alice in Wonderland, *1865*

*The pig-baby in* Alice in Wonderland. *Lewis Carroll invented a trick stamp case in which a baby turns into a pig. 'If that doesn't surprise you,' he said, 'why, I suppose you wouldn't be surprised if your own Mother-in-Law suddenly turned into a Gyroscope!'*

## THE PIG'S WHO'S WHO

### A Gallery Of Children's Book Pig Heroes

◆

**Aunt Pettitoes, Alexander and Berkshire Pigwig** These pigs make their debuts in Beatrix Potter's *The Tale of Pigling Bland.*

**Bertie** the pig is the star of *Bertie's Escapade*, a story by *The Wind in the Willows* author Kenneth Grahame, published posthumously in 1949. His motto is 'Deeds, not grunts', and he encourages two reluctant rabbits, Peter and Benjie, to join him on an unsuccessful carol-singing sortie.

**Freddy** appears in the picture books of American author, Walter Rollin Brooks, with illustrations by Kurt Wiese, published from the 1930s to the 1950s.

Freddy is 'the smallest and cleverest pig' on Mr Bean's farm.

**Gub Gub** The ever-hungry pig in the *Doctor Dolittle* stories written and illustrated by Hugh Lofting during the period 1922–1948, much teased by Jip the dog. Gub Gub is the subject of one of Lofting's books – *Gub Gub's Book* (1932), in which he dreams up 'A History of Eating'.

**Hen Wen** The pig gifted with prophetic powers under the care of Taran the Assistant Pig-Keeper appears in Lloyd Alexander's *The Book of Three* (1964) and *The High King* (1968).

*Dr Dolittle's Gub Gub in character-istic pose (ie: eating), pauses to prod a Marchioness.*

*Winnie-the-Pooh's pal Piglet feels suddenly deflated in this drawing by E. H. Shepard.*

*Beatrix Potter's Little Pig Robinson races along the beach at 'Stymouth' before his epic voyage.*

**Little Pig Robinson** The eponymous hero of Beatrix Potter's *The Tale of Little Pig Robinson* (1930) was based on her recollections of seeing a pig on board a ship in Devon.

**Piglet** One of the nursery animals of the real-life Christopher Robin, he first appeared in the pages of A. A. Milne's *Winnie-the-Pooh* (1926) with illustrations by E. H. Shepard.

**Pigling Bland** Another of Beatrix Potter's piggy characters who stars in *The Tale of Pigling Bland* (1913).

**Piggly** A less well-known pig who features in Angusine Macgregor's *Piggly Plays Truant* (1946).

**Pig Plantagenet** Pig Plantagenet is the hero of Allen Andrews' story of the same name (1980), illustrated by Michael Foreman.

**Pigwig** The pig (with the same name as a real pig owned by Beatrix Potter) appears in stories and illustrations by John Dyke, including *Pigwig and the Pirates* (1979).

**Anthony Henrypottery Luxulyan Prettypig** Though tiny, Anthony stands head and shoulders above all other fictional pigs by virtue of his long name. He is the train-obsessed china pig in Mary and Rowland Emett's *Anthony and Antimacassar* (1943). Antimacassar is the pink railway engine on the Grand Royal Steam Joint-Branch Railway under the command of Head-Chief-Driver Mister Stuffingbox.

*Anthony Henrypottery Luxulyan Prettypig meets Mister Stuffingbox as he clears the bats from Antimacassar's funnel.*

**Sam Pig** is the central character in the very popular stories by Alison Uttley, the author of the Little Grey Rabbit books, illustrated, (1941–1960), by A. F. Kennedy. Sam lives in a cottage with two brothers, Tom and Bill and his sister Ann.

**The Three Little Pigs** The pigs of this traditional story, popularised by the Walt Disney cartoon, also appear in Leonard Leslie Brooke's *The Story of the Three Little Pigs* (1904), *The Golden Goose Book* (1905) and *This Little Pig Went to Market* (1922).

**Wilbur** is the runt rescued from slaughter in E. B. White's *Charlotte's Webb* (1952), illustrated by Garth Williams. His survival is extended when he is befriended by Charlotte the spider who declares him to be 'Terrific' by spinning the word into her web.

*Hey diddle-diddle, the pig and the fiddle . . . Alison Uttley's Sam Pig in* Sam Pig Goes to Market *(1941), drawn by A. F. Kennedy.*

## PIGS IN NURSERY RHYMES

### The Sow Came In With The Saddle

The sow came in with the saddle.
The little pig rocked the cradle,
The dish jumped up on the table
To see the pot swallow the ladle.

### Tom, Tom The Piper's Son

Tom, Tom the Piper's son,
Stole a pig and away he run;
The pig was eat
And Tom was beat
And Tom went howling
    down the street.

Beatrix Potter's version, sung by Pigling Bland, is:

Tom, Tom the Piper's son,
    stole a pig and away he ran!
But all the tune
    that he could play,
was 'Over the hills and far away!'

*Pigs' pettitoes? A graphic – and somewhat surreal – variation on* This Little Piggy Went to Market.

This little pig went to market.
—This little pig staid at home.
This little pig had a bit of roast beef.
This little pig had none.
This little pig said, —
"Tweak! tweak! tweak! Mamma, I want some!"

### This Little Piggy Went To Market

This little piggy went to market,
This little piggy stayed home,
This little piggy had roast beef,
This little piggy had none,
And this little piggy cried,
*Wee, wee, wee, wee, wee . . .*
All the way home.

### To Market, To Market

To market, to market, to buy
    a fat pig,
Home again, home again,
    jiggety-jig;
Ride to the market to buy
    a fat hog,
Home again, home again,
    jiggcty-jog.

### Grandfa' Grig

Grandfa' Grig
Had a pig,
In a field of clover;
Piggie died,
Grandfa' cried,
And all the fun was over.

65

# PIGS IN VERSE

### P Stands For Pig

P stands for Pig, as I remarked
before,
A second cousin to the Huge Wild
Boar.
But Pigs are civilised, while Huge
Wild Boars
Live savagely, at random, out of
doors,
And in their coarse contempt of
dainty foods,
Subsist on Truffles, which they
find in woods.
Not so the cultivated Pig, who feels
The need of several courses at
his meals,
But wrongly thinks it does not
matter whether
He takes them one by one or all
together.
Hence, Pigs devour, from lack of
self respect,
What Epicures would certainly
eject.

MORAL:
Learn from the Pig to take
whatever Fate
Or Elder Persons heap on your
plate.

*Hilaire Belloc*
*A Bad Child's Book of Beasts, 1940*

### Anonymous Limerick

There was an old man of Antigua,
Whose wife said,
'My dear, what a pig you are!'
He replied, 'O my queen,
In manners you mean,
Or do you refer to my fig-u-a?'

### The Barrister's Dream

He dreamed that he stood
in a shadowy Court,
Where the Snark, with a glass
in its eye,
Dressed in gown, bands, and wig,
was defending a pig
On the charge of deserting its sty.

*Lewis Carroll* The Hunting of the Snark, *1876*

### The Pig-Tale

. . . Suddenly the Professor started as if he had been electrified. 'Why, I had nearly forgotten the most important part of the entertainment! The Other Professor is to recite a Tale of a Pig – I mean a Pig-Tale,' he corrected himself. 'It has Introductory Verses at the beginning, and at the end.'

There was a Pig, that sat alone
Beside a ruined Pump:
By day and night he made his moan –
It would have stirred a heart of stone
To see him wring his hoofs
and groan,
Because he could not jump.

A certain Camel heard him shout –
A Camel with a hump.
'Oh, is it Grief, or is it Gout?
What is this bellowing about?'
That Pig replied, with quivering
snout,
'Because I cannot jump!'

That Camel scanned him,
    dreamy-eyed.
  'Methinks you are too plump.
I never knew a Pig so wide –
That wobbled so from side to side –
Who could, however much he tried,
    Do such a thing as *jump*!

'Yet mark those trees, two miles
    away,
  All clustered in a clump:
If you could trot there twice a day,
Nor ever pause for rest or play,
In the far future – Who can say? –
    You may be fit to jump.'

(Unfortunately, the Pig ignores the
Camel's advice and follows that of a
passing Frog who persuades him to
copy his leaping – which sadly proves
fatal.)
*Lewis Carroll*
Sylvie and Bruno Concluded, *1893*

*Mome raths in their natural habitat,*
*with toves and borogroves.*

## The Enigma Of The Mome Rath

The great pig lover, Lewis Carroll,
introduces pigs into many of his
works, but in *Through the Looking-
Glass* he poses a piggy problem:

'You seem very clever at explaining
words, Sir,' said Alice. 'Would you
kindly tell me the meaning of a poem
called *Jabberwocky*?'

'Let's hear it,' said Humpty
Dumpty. 'I can explain all the poems
that ever were invented – and a good
many that haven't been invented just
yet.'

This sounded hopeful, so Alice
repeated the first verse:

'Twas brillig, and the slithy toves
  Did gyre and gimble in the wabe:
All mimsy were the borogroves,
  And the mome raths outgrabe'

Humpty Dumpty explains that '. . .
a *rath* is a sort of green pig'; but in an
early version of *Jabberwocky*, his little-
known *Stanza of Anglo-Saxon Poetry*
written for the amusement of his
brothers and sisters in 1855 – fifteen
years before *Looking-Glass* – Carroll
had explained *rath* as 'a species of
land turtle'. It is, in fact an Irish
name for a fortified enclosure, leaving
us with the puzzle of whether Carroll
or Humpty Dumpty got it right. Is a
rath a green pig? One would rather
hope so . . .

*Illustrator William Foster captures the moment when the bargain is struck between the pussycat and the pig in Edward Lear's* The Owl and the Pussycat.

## Edward Lear's Nonsense Pigs

There was an Old Person of Anerley,
Whose conduct was strange and
    unmannerly;
  He rushed down the Strand,
    with a pig in each hand,
But returned in the evening to
    Anerley.

A Book of Nonsense, *1846*

There was an old man of Messina
Whose daughter was named
    Opsibeena;
  She wore a small wig,
    and rode out on a pig,
To the perfect delight of Messina.

More Nonsense, *1872*

### P

P was a pig
Who was not very big
But his tail was too curly,
And that made him surly.
P!
Cross little Pig!

Nonsense Alphabet, *1871*

There was a Young Lady of Bute,
Who played on a silver-gilt flute;
  She played several jigs,
    to her uncle's white pigs,
That amusing Young Lady of Bute.

. . . And there in a wood a Piggy-wig
    stood
With a ring at the end of his nose . . .

'Dear Pig, are you willing
    to sell for one shilling
Your ring?' Said the Piggy, 'I will.'
So they took it away, and were
    married next day
By the Turkey who lives
    on the hill . .

Nonsense Songs, *1871*

## The Pig And Whistle: Musical Pigs

Pigs may whistle, but they ha'e an ill mouth for't.

*Scottish proverb*

Tom with his pipe did play
    with such skill,
That those who heard him could
    never keep still;
As soon as he played they began
    for to dance,
Even pigs on their hind legs would
    after him prance.

*Traditional rhyme*

Pigs said to like music, and singing and dancing pigs appear in the humorous folktales of several countries – usually by way of emphasising their alleged ungainly movement and total lack of an ear for music. But pigs and boars have been the subject of many traditional songs and such works as Sir Francis Cowley Burnard's *The Pig Song* (1877), T. C. Tweedie's *The Pigsticking Song* (1913) and Colin Hand's *The Pig's Tail* (1958). *Piggies* by George Harrison appears on The Beatles' 'White Album' (1968).

## A Pig Puzzle: Turning A Pig Into A Sty

In an article in *Vanity Fair* (29 March 1879) Lewis Carroll presented the word game he called 'Doublets'. In it, by changing one letter at a time, one can produce a chain of words connecting two given words. In one of his examples, it is possible in five moves to make 'PIG' into 'STY':

*Solution to Pig Puzzle:*
PIG WIG WAG WAY SAY STY

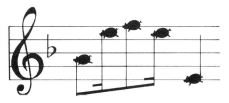

## A Pig Opera

Ernest Henry Griset (1844–1907), a French-born artist who settled in England, devised a piggy opera – not exactly Pigoletto or Wagner's Pig Ring Cycle, but 'The Hog Family: An Operetta for the Drawing Room'. Here is an excerpt:

QUARTETTE
**Mr Big Boar:** Grumph!
**Mrs Sow:** Umph!
**Master Pig:** Ooink
**Master Piggywig:** Oonk, oonk, oonk!

*They perceive an acorn and rush towards it*
**All:** Gruooinkurmph-urmph-urmph!

*Enter suddenly* **Piggywiggling**
**Piggywigling:** Week, weeeek, weeeek!

*They gather round him with great affection*
**Piggywigling:** (*Imploringly*) Oooweeeek!

*A shot is heard in the distance*
**Mr Big Boar:** Grrrrruuuumph!

*Exeunt rapidly in procession*
CURTAIN

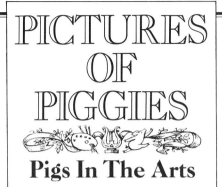

# PICTURES OF PIGGIES

## Pigs In The Arts

THE PIG HAS BEEN THOUGHT a highly fitting subject for the brushes of painters since the Neolithic artist responsible for the cave paintings at Altamira in Spain turned his hand to the depiction of wild boars in about 4000 BC. Some painters have even seemed to justify the piggy associations of their names by portraying pigs: William Hogarth was adept at painting rumbustious feasts, while his *Marriage à la Mode* (1743), now in the National Gallery, London, includes a detail showing a hound seizing a pig's head from a dining table. In our own time the eminent British artist Francis Bacon has fulfilled the promise of his name by becoming the master of still lifes featuring meat carcases.

In the Middle Ages, the 'occupations of the months' were a popular theme for the monkish painters of manuscript miniatures: many magnificent examples show pigs fattened by feeding with acorns, generally in October, and their subsequent slaughter, traditionally in November, for food for the Christmas table and to provide sustenance throughout winter. Often these scenes are richly painted and spirited in their depiction of the fattened pig meeting his end by a belt from a mallet that makes a polo player's resemble a tack hammer. They also give the best clue as to the appearance of the medieval pig, which resembles his wild forebears, or foreboars, with long hind legs and a spiked back, rather than the plump, rounded form of the pig with which we are familiar. Boar hunting is also often shown in manuscript illustrations – that representing the month of December in the famous *Très Riches Heures du Duc de Berry*, for example, has a boar that has been felled, though only after being savaged by no fewer than nine hunting dogs. Boars and pigs were also used in paintings of the Middle Ages to symbolize such earthly vices as gluttony and licentiousness: the works of Hieronymus Bosch (*c.* 1450–1516) contain such images. Albrecht Dürer (1471–1528), though elevated to the rank of Court Painter to the Emperors Maximillian and Charles V, did not consider pigs beneath him: the pigs and piglets in his engraving of *The Prodigal Son* were clearly drawn from life by a man who knew and understood them.

Both Rubens (1577–1640) and Rembrandt (1606–69) numbered pigs among their subjects, as did the English painter of rustic

scenes, George Morland (1763–1804). Thomas Bewick (1753–1828), whose low opinion of pigs we have already read, nevertheless produced numerous skilful woodcuts of them. To achieve the realism he demanded in his painting, *Cottage Girl with Pigs*, Thomas Gainsborough (1727–88) had live pigs brought to the studio in his Pall Mall house, presenting a strange scene that was noted by a visiting oboeist called John Parke. In 1782 the painting was bought for 100 guineas (£105) by Sir Joshua Reynolds, to whom Gainsborough remarked, 'I think myself highly honoured and much obliged to you for this singular mark of favour; I may freely say I have brought my pigs to a fine market!'

Felicien Rops' *Pornocrates* (1896), an etching and aquatint of a nude

*Albrecht Dürer's engraving of the Prodigal Son as a swineherd surrounded by pigs and piglets.*

woman with a pig on a lead, stands out as one of the most bizarre pictures of pigs, while among other notable nineteenth-century pig paintings one might include Jean-François Millet's *Death of a Pig* (1869) – but perhaps pass over it quickly as it is a gloomy French rural scene showing a reluctant pig being dragged to its death. Stanley Spencer's *Rickett's Farm, Cookham Dene* (1938), now in the Tate Gallery, strikes a cheerier note, with pigs and piglets happily feeding in ramshackle sties, and present day artists of the eminence of Henry Moore and such popular naive and primitive painters as Beryl Cook have continued to find pigs an enduring source of artistic inspiration.

*Pen and ink and wash drawing of a friendly pig by Sir Peter Paul Rubens. Although, like Dürer, Rubens was a court painter, he displayed considerable affection for porcine subjects.*

*(Left) Felicien Rops' quirky* Pornocrates. *(Above) A cap badge found at Middleham Castle showing Richard III's emblem of a boar.*

## The Heraldic Boar

The boar has long been regarded as a 'sovereign beast', its ferocity making it ideally suited as an emblem of courage and power. For this reason it was chosen as the badge of the Roman Twentieth Legion, and in modern times of various regiments. One of the most famous men to use the boar on his coat of arms was Richard III, giving rise to the rhyme in which he and his consorts are referred to by their heraldic devices:

> The Cat, the Rat and Lovell
> our Dogge
> Rule all England under
> an Hogge.

The boar has also been used as a punning motif by various members of families with the surname, Bacon, and, less obviously, by the Vere family, because *verres* is Latin for boar: Sir Francis Vere's tomb in Westminster Abbey has a boar on it, as do those of John Wildbore in Kirkby and the Gammon family in Chester. In Hereford Cathedral a swinish procession aptly marches round the tomb of Precentor Swinfield, while a solitary pig supplies him with a footrest.

### Pig Inn-Signia

In towns and in rural areas in Britain the pig has left his mark – as an inn sign. Inn names such as *The Three Boars* and others with boars probably have an heraldic origin. Richard III's arms, which featured a white boar, were said to have been swiftly repainted blue, the Earl of Oxford's colour, when Henry VII acceded to the throne.

Perhaps the commonest of all pig inn signs, *The Pig and Whistle*, has caused the greatest controversy as to its origin. Among the explanations have been that it comes from: *Pix and Housel* (archaic words for the Host used in Christian services and the practice of 'shriving', or paying penance); *Pige-Washael* (an old salutation to the Virgin Mary); *Piggin of Wassail* (a festive drink – 'piggin' was a small pot); *Pig* (meaning a 'pot') and *Whistle* (meaning 'small change') or from a joking reference to a crudely-painted sign that was actually supposed to depict a bear with a staff. In fact, the simplest explanation is the most likely, and the sign really is meant to show a pig and a whistle, since there are many legends relating to musical pigs and church carvings of pigs playing bagpipes were once common –

*(Left) An inn sign in South Molton Street, London, one of the many swinish names for inns.*

and these would have been the most familiar source of inspiration for early inn sign painters.

Other piggy inn names include *The Hampshire Hog*, *The Hog and Donkey*, *The Hog in Armour*, *The Hog* (or *Pig*) *in the Pound*, *The Black Pig*, *The Blue Pig*, *The Little Pig*, *The Pig and Butcher*, *The Pretty Pigs* and *The Sow and Pigs*.

## Pigs In Church

Pigs appeared in carvings and stained glass in medieval churches in Europe for a variety of reasons. They were used to satirize the behaviour and especially the vices of men and women, to indicate morals, to illustrate everyday activities in rural areas, and sometimes just for the amusement of portraying pigs engaged in human pursuits.

There was also clearly a good deal of affection in many images, particularly in the very commonly featured one of a sow and piglets. Sometimes

the message was more complex: in Rouen Cathedral, for example, a carving shows a woman emptying a basket of marguerite blossoms in front of a pig. The obscure symbolism of this derives from the fact that the Latin for pearl is *margarita* and it thus signifies the biblical injunction, 'do not cast pearls before swine'. Pigs in church were often shown playing musical instruments: one in Winchester Cathedral is an authentic 'pig and whistle', while others perform on bagpipes and harps and even, in a church in Vra, Denmark, on a guitar.

## Pottery Pigs

Although the name of a certain painter of Greek vases in about 470 BC has not come down to us, his images of pigs are so characteristic and beautiful that he is known simply as 'The Pig Painter'.

The very origin of the word 'porcelain' derives from an association

*A treasure trove of piggy collectibles, including pigs in (and on) pots and ashtrays, and proving that even if you can't make a silk purse out of a sow's ear, you can squeeze two pigs into a poke.*

with pigs, albeit a rather convoluted and vulgar one: the Italian word, *porcellana*, literally meant 'sow's vulva', and this was the name given to the cowrie shell from its resemblance to that part of the sow's anatomy; porcelain, in turn, was originally so-called after its shell-like finish.

The traditional 'Sussex Pig' was made in the 19th century at the Cadborough pottery. It was fashioned in such a way that it could sit down, its removable head being used to drink wedding toasts, with the inevitable

*A piggy bank – perhaps the most familiar and popular of all representations of pigs.*

comment that the drinker had consumed a 'hogshead of ale'.

Ceramic piggy banks, originally made so that they had to be smashed to retrieve their contents, probably date from 18th century and are popular the world over – though nowhere more so than in Denmark where there are even piggy bank museums.

At one time that most cannibalistic of folk art objects, the butcher's shop statuette of a 'butcher pig' in his striped apron, preparing to carve his brothers and sisters, was a familiar image in the windows of British butchers; it is now a rarity.

## Pigs On Paper

After the Reformation, King Henry VIII had notepaper made for himself with a watermark depicting a pig wearing a tiara – an emblematical representation of a supposedly brutish creature in a bejewelled crown, which was intended as a satirical attack on the Pope.

## Other Representations of Pigs

Statues of pigs are rare, but not unknown. In the Museo Nazzionale, Naples there is a fine Roman bronze of a jolly leaping piglet, found in Herculaneaum and dating from the first half of the 1st century, and in the Hall of the Grocer's Company in the City of London there is a statue of St Anthony and his pig.

Coins dating back to ancient times have featured boars and pigs, a tradition which persists in the coinage of such countries as Ireland and Bermuda.

In countries where pigs were revered, models of them were frequently buried in tombs: archaeologists have unearthed magnificent ancient Chinese grave objects, including whole stiesful of model pigs, especially from the Han period (roughly 200 years either side of the birth of Christ). Egyptian and Celtic burials also often contained miniature representations of pigs and boars.

*A heavyweight paperweight: an early 1900s' Viennese statuette of a sow and piglets.*

Boar hunting was widely depicted on medieval tapestries, some of them brilliantly executed, such as the Devonshire Hunting Tapestries (1430–35), now in the Victoria & Albert Museum, in which men armed with spears and hunting dogs pursue a tusked boar.

Oriental pig-lovers have exercised their craft in creating pig puppets in Java, and in Japan *netsuke* – wooden or ivory toggles used as fasteners – frequently depict wild boars.

The pig continues to be a subject for artists and new media have been exploited in recent times, giving rise to comic postcards, photographs and greetings cards, posters and album covers. Among the most imaginative of the latter is that of the pop group Pink Floyd's *Animals* which has a photograph of a Dutch-made inflatable pig tethered over London's Battersea Power Station. In the fantasy world of rock music, pigs really *do* fly . . .

*Danish bacon – an industry and an important component of the language.*

**I**N A COUNTRY SUCH AS Denmark, where pigs have a crucial place in the economy, it is not surprising to find a huge number of pig words – the Danish dictionary has 24 columns of words relating to pig, sow, hog, boar and swine. Danish pig words and phrases include:

**Pig feathers** Bedding straw
**Pigs' ears** The name of a certain kind of biscuit
**Pig** A small train on a branch line
**Pig** A vaulting horse used in gymnastics

## Names Given To The Smallest Pig In A Litter

The most common name for the smallest pig in a litter in Britain and the USA is the 'runt', but as recently as the 1920s, a number of dialect words were also used in different parts of Britain and Ireland, among them:

*Bonneen/bonnine* – Co. Cork
*Cad* – Essex
*Cadman* – Somerset
*Crink* – Breconshire
*Darling* – Hampshire, Ireland
*Dawlin* – Surrey and Sussex
*Derlin* – Berkshire
*Dilling* – Buckinghamshire
*Doll* – New Forest
*Dolling* – Sussex
*Dorling* – Surrey
*Harry-pig* – Aberdeenshire
*Nestle-tripe/trype* – Somerset
*Nisgull* – Worcestershire
*Parson's pig* – Somerset and Dorset
*Piggywhidden* – Cornwall
*Ratlin* – Montgomeryshire
*Ratling/reckling/rickling* – Shropshire
*Reckling* – Lincolnshire
*Rit/ritling/ruckling* – Cheshire
*Squeaker* – Somerset
*Tantony pig* – Kent
*Wossett* – New Forest
*Wreg* – Scotland

## Some Piggy Plants

Some plants are connected with pigs because they are used as fodder, and others because of their appearance:

**Pig-in-the-hedge** Blackthorn
**Pig lily** Aurum lily
**Pig rush or pig weed** Knotgrass, fed to pigs '... when they are sicke and will not eate their meate'
*John Gerard* Herball, *1597*

**Pig's bubble** Cow parsnip, also known as 'pig's cole' and 'pig's flop'
**Pig's foot** Birdsfoot trefoil
**Pig's ear** 'Biting stonecrop'
**Pig's eye** Cuckoo flower
**Pig's mouth** Toadflax, also called 'pig's chops'
**Pig's nose** A variety of apple; also the rose hip
**Pigtail** Goosegrass
**Swine's snout** Dandelion

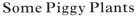

## Some Popular Pig Breeds

Berkshire
Dorset Gold Tip
Gloucester Old Spot
Landrace
Large Black
Large White Yorkshire
Little Black Berkshire
Middle White Yorkshire
Saddleback
Suffolk
Tamworth
Wessex Saddleback

## SOME PIGGY PHRASES

**To baste your bacon** To strike or scourge

**To have boiled pig at home** To be master of one's own house. It apparently derives from a now forgotten story.

**Born at Hogs-Norton** Ill-mannered, from the proverbial saying, 'I think thou wast born at Hoggs-Norton where piggs play upon the organs'. Hock-Norton in Leicestershire had an organist called Piggs.

**Bring home the bacon** To achieve success, or material rewards

**To bring one's pigs to a pretty market** To make a bad bargain

**As drunk as Davy's sow** Recorded as early as 1671, this phrase is said to have derived from an anecdote about David Lloyd, a Hereford innkeeper, who kept a six-legged sow as a curiosity at his inn. One day his wife got drunk and lay down in the sow's sty. David showed visitors in and said, 'There is a sow for you! Did you ever see the like?' to which a visitor replied, 'Well, it is the drunkenest sow I ever beheld!'

**To be driving hogs (or pigs) to market** Snoring loudly

**Go the whole hog** This phrase, which suggests doing something thoroughly, perhaps comes from the use of the word 'hog', meaning ten cents in the United States or a shilling in England; to 'go the whole hog' thus meant to splash out, or spend extravagantly. It was popularised during Andrew Jackson's presidential campaign of 1828 and used in England after about 1840. A 'whole-hogger' is a person who will see some enterprise through to the bitter end.

**Go to pigs and whistles** Scottish slang meaning to be financially ruined

**To hear as a hog in harvest** 'In one ear and out the other':

If you call hogs out of the harvest stubble, they will just lift up their heads to listen, and fall back to their shack (stubble feeding) again
*Giles Firmin* Real Christian, *1670*

**Pig Latin** A 'secret language', used among children, in which the beginnings of words are placed at the end followed by 'ay', in order to make it difficult for the uninitiated to follow; 'pig' thus becomes 'igpay'. The connection with pigs may be that a pig's grunt is just as unintelligible.

*Grunnio ergo sum ...*

*A 'hog on ice' – less stable than the one implied in the phrase. An illustration from Alison Uttley's* Sam Pig and the Singing Gate *(1955).*

**High on the hog** Living in profligate style – as one would if feasting off a whole pig

**As independent as a hog on ice** Hogs on ice are clearly not in control, so it is paradoxical that the phrase means self-confident. It possibly has a Scottish origin related to the heavy – and hence solidly reliable – 'hog' used in the sport of curling.

**Piggy-in-the-middle** Caught between two disputing factions, after the children's game of this name in which a ball is tossed between two players with a third, the 'piggy', attempting to intercept it

**Hog and hominy** In America, pork and maize

**Male chauvinist pigs** The battle-cry of the feminist movement; 'chauvinist' comes from the name of the French soldier of the Napoleonic period, Nicolas Chauvin, and means fanatically patriotic – or in this instance, irrationally believing in the superiority of the male sex. Whether or not one holds with this notion, it is surely unfair to drag pigs into the argument . . .

**On the pig's back** Lucky; perhaps derived from folktales in which people rode on magic pigs

**Pigs in clover** Behaving improperly with one's money – as reckless as a pig set loose in a clover field might be

**Hog in armour** A rough person in fine clothes

**A pig of my own sow** The result of one's own action — self-induced

**Saving your bacon** Looking after oneself – as the bacon that a family lived on during winter would be cherished:

But here I say the Turks were
    much mistaken,
Who hating hogs, yet wished to
    save their bacon.
*Byron* Don Juan, *1818–20, vii.42*

**Please the pigs** If at all possible; it is said to come from 'please the pixies', but this is unlikely

**Pig iron** So-called because molten iron passes down a channel (a 'sow') and off into branches forming 'pigs', named after their resemblance to piglets feeding at a sow

**A still sow** A cunning or selfish person, as in the proverbial phrase, 'still swine eats all the draff':

We do not act that often jest
    and laugh;
'Tis old, but true,
    'Still swine eats all the draff.'
*Shakespeare* Merry Wives of Windsor, *IV.ii*

**To stare like a stuck pig** Staring in astonishment – as indeed a pig that has been stuck might

**A pig's whisper** No time at all – something that is over as quickly as a pig's grunt

**When pigs fly** Never. The earliest references to this expression are 17th century. John Withals, the author of the *Shorte Dictionarie for Younge Begynners* (1553), declared 'Pigs flie in the ayre with their tayles forward . . .'

# HOW TO DRAW A PIG

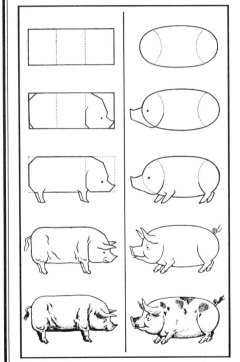

# A PIGTIONARY OF OBSCURE PIG WORDS

**Adeps**  Pork fat, lard

**Axunge**  Pig fat

**Barrow**  A castrated boar

**Bartholomew pig**  A pig sold at Bartholomew Fair, held in Smithfield, London, from the 12th–19th century

**Chitterling**  The small intestines of a pig – often fried or stuffed like a sausage. The word was also used to describe a kind of ornamental braid, the shape of which it resembled.

**Cingular**  A wild boar in its fifth year

**Creep**  A safe place for piglets to feed without the danger of the sow rolling over and crushing them

**Drift**  A group of domesticated pigs

**Galt**  A boar or male pig

**Grice**  A young boar or pig – especially a suckling pig, or its meat

**Griskin**  The lean part of a loin of pork

**Grunter**  A pig. In the 18th century, 'grunter's gig' was described as a dish of 'smoaked hog's face'.

**Gruntle**  The snout of a pig, or the sound made by a pig

**Gruntling**  A small grunter, or young pig

**Hoggaster**  A boar in its third year

**Hogget**  A boar in its second year

**Hogling**  A young pig

**Hog-money**  Bermudan coins, so-called because they had an image of a hog on them

**Hog-reeve**  A New England official whose duties included assessing damages caused by stray pigs

*Birds of a feather flock together – and so do pigs: a 'drift' of swine.*

*An authentic 'hog-wallow' – complete with hog, wallowing.*

**Hog-wallows** Deep puddles occurring during rainstorms in undulating American prairie country

**Hogwash** Swill from a brewery or kitchen, fed to pigs – hence any inferior garbage

**Marcassin** In heraldry, a young wild boar, depicted as having a straight rather than twisted tail of old boar

**Misosyst** A pig-hater

**My Sow's Pigged** An archaic card game

**Pig** A segment of an orange

**Pig cote** A pigsty or pig-pen

**Pigdom** A realm of pigs

**Piggicide** One who kills pigs

**Pigless** Without pigs

**Pig-man/Pig-wife** Scottish crockery sellers

**Pig-sconce** A pigheaded person

**Pigsney** A term of endearment, like 'darling', derived from 'pig's eye'

**Pigtail** A twisted rope of tobacco

**Pigtaker** A purveyor of pigs – at

one time an official position in the British royal household

**Pig-puzzle** A gate that swings both ways

**Plobby** The sound of a pig eating, coined by P. G. Wodehouse in *Pig-hoo-o-o-o-ey!* to describe a pig eating, 'a sort of gulpy, gurgly, plobby, squishy, woffle-some sound'

**Porconologist** One who writes about pigs

**Sanglier** A wild boar separated from its sounder (qv)

**Shoat/Shote** A young pig, weaned, but under a year old

**Sounder** A herd of wild pigs

**Sow** In America, a moveable shed used by miners; in Scotland and northern England, a haystack

**Suidian/Suilline** Pertaining to swine

**Suine** Imitation butter made from pig lard

**Tusker** A wild boar

# PIGSLANG

The pig is one of the most prolific animals in slang – not only in English: in French, for example, a dirty trick is a *tour de cochon*, slapdash work is *travail de cochon*, if one is dead drunk, one is said to be *plein comme un cochon*, and to talk dirty is to *dire des cochonneries*. Here is a selection of English pigslang:

**Bacon, bacon bonce, bacon-brains, bacon-slicer, chaw-bacon** Terms of abuse aimed at rustics, from the fact that in rural areas bacon was the commonly eaten meat

**Bacon and eggs** Rhyming slang for legs

**Bacon tree** A pig

**China Street Pig** A Bow Street Runner, the precursors of the police. China Street was a slang term for Bow Street.

**Grunting peck** Bacon

**Ham** An amateurish actor, from 'ham-bone', American slang for a novice performer

**Hog** A student of St John's College, Cambridge. This expression possibly came from Anglo Saxon 'hogan', meaning to study. The bridge separating the two parts of the college was known as the Bridge of Grunts, and the trimmings on the college gowns as 'crackling'.

**Hog** A native of Hampshire. It is by no means used as a term of abuse: the Castle at Winchester in Hampshire has a hog weathervane, and 'The Hogs' is the nickname of the Hampshire cricket team.

**Hog** A coin, in England confusingly used to mean sixpence, a shilling (most commonly), half a crown or five shillings, and in the USA a ten cent piece, or dime

**Hog** A heavy drug-user

**Hog** A Hell's Angel's Harley Davidson motorcycle

**Hog caller** A scream

**Hog fat** A nuisance

**Hog shearing** Much ado about nothing. 'Great cry and little wool', as the devil said when he sheared the hogs in the medieval mystery play, *David and Abigail.*

**Hog-tied** Pinned down

**Hogwash** 'Rot-gut' liquor, or rubbish

**Hog wild** Berserk (US)

**In pig** Pregnant

**Never in a pig's ear** Never at all, from rhyming slang for 'never in a year'

**Pickled pork** Rhyming slang for 'talk'

**Pig** A policeman. Although its use became widespread in the 1960s, it dates from the early 19th century.

**Pig** A useless horse

*If you see one pig or two,*
*Depends upon your point of view.*
*But who'd say this cop's name is mud*
*If he saves piggy from the flood?*

**Pig** A sixpenny piece

**Pig/Pork** A tailor's term for a spoiled garment

**Pig** A promiscuous woman

**Pig** A straight, establishment type of person

**Pig** A worker in a printing office

**Pig** Recent British army slang for the Humber 10-ton armoured personnel-carrier, especially in Northern Ireland – probably from its lumbering appearance

**Pig and roast** Rhyming slang for 'toast'

**Pig and Tinder Box** Elephant and Castle – a humorous description of the inn sign

**Pig and Whistle** The nickname of the Highland Light Infantry, which had an elephant and a hunting horn on its regimental badge

**Pig brother** A black police informant

**Piggies** Baby talk for toes, from the nursery rhyme, 'This Little Piggy'

**Pigging** Engaged in sexual intercourse

**Pig heaven** A police station, or a fantasy land for greedy people

**Pig ignorant** Extremely ignorant

**Pig Islander** A New Zealander

**Pig it** To live in squalor

**Pig meat** A prostitute

**Pig mouth** A term of abuse

**Pig out** To gourmandise to excess (US expression)

**Pig party** A homosexual orgy or 'gang bang'

**Pig-penny-horse** A money bos – though usually more horse-like than pig shaped

**Pigs!** An expression of disgust, akin to 'ugh!'

**Pigs aft** Naval officers

**Pigs are up** A Second World War expression meaning 'barrage balloons have been launched', derived from the pig-like appearance of the balloons

**Pig's ear** A modern expression meaning a mess, which was possibly rhyming slang for 'smear', or a euphemism for a 'pig's arse'

**Pig's ear** Rhyming slang for beer

**Pig's ear** A type of pastry

**Pig's eye** The ace of diamonds

**Pig's fry** Rhyming slang for 'tie'

**Pig's-head negus** 19th-century naval slang for soup

**Pigshit** Garbage

**Pigskin** A saddle

**Pig-sticker** A bayonet

**Pig sty** A police station

**Pig style** Filthy style

**Pig-yoke** A nautical measuring instrument

**Pork pie** Rhyming slang for 'a lie'

**Rabbit and pork** Rhyming slang for talk, as in the Chas & Dave song, *Rabbit*

**Sow's baby** Sixpence

CARBONIQUE'S PATENT **INFLATING POWDERS,** FOR PROMOTING SPHERICITY.

## Pig People

In 1896 *The Times* recorded that a Mr Pigg was changing his name to Pegg. Most people with piggy names, however, are content to live with them. Among them are:

**Bacon**

**Boar**

**Galt/Gault/Gaute** From the Middle English *galte* or *gaute*, a boar

**Grice/Griss** From the Old Norman *griss*, a pig

**Hogg** From the Old English, *hogg*, a pig – for example, Quintin Hogg, Lord Hailsham

**Hogsflesh** A surname found in Sussex

**Kellogg** From 'kill hog', a hog butcher

**Pigge**

**Purcell** In French *purcel* means a little pig

**Seward** Sowherd

**Swinart** Swineherd

**Swinburne** Swine stream

**Weatherhog** A Lincolnshire name meaning male pig

**Wilber** Wild Boar

**Willgrass/Willgress** From *Wildegris*, a wild pig

**GASPAR GRISWOLD BACON**

## Pig Places

**Barley (Lancashire)** From the Old English, *bar*, a boar

**Barlow (Derbyshire, Durham and Yorkshire)** As above

**Barwell (Leicestershire)** As above

**Boar's Hill (Berkshire)**

**Boarzell (Sussex)** Boar's pasture

**Borseford (Herefordshire)** Same derivation as Barley

**Bos Ait (Surrey)** Same derivation as Barley

**Bowerswain (Dorset)** As Barley

**Byro Hills** Boar's hills

**Hog's back (Surrey)**

**Muckross, Fife** Celtic for boar's promontory

**Somborne (Hampshire)** Wild boar stream

**Swilland (Suffolk)** Land where pigs were kept

**Swinbrook (Oxfordshire)**

**Swinburn (Northumberland)**

**Swinden (Yorkshire)**

**Swindon (Wiltshire)** Pig hill

**Swinefleet (Humberside)** Pig stream

**Swinscoe (Staffordshire)** Pig wood

**Swinside (North Yorkshire)** Pig headland

**Swineshead (Bedfordshire)** Homestead where pigs were reared

**Swinton (Borders)** Pig farm

**Toller Porcorum (Dorset)** Noted for its pig population. Hence:
'Pon my life an' honner,
As I was gowine to Toller,
I met a pig without a wig,
'Pon my life an' honner!

**Wild Boar's Fell (Cumbria)**

## PIG TRIVIA

### Pigs In The Theatre, In Movies, And On Television

Pigs have featured in the titles – and sometimes the stories – of a number of theatrical performances and films, including: Andy Warhol's *Pork*, *Porkies*, *Dr Dolittle*, Pasolini's *Porcile* (US: *Pigpen*; UK: *Pigsty*), *Futz*, *Three Little Pigs*, *A Shocking Accident* and *A Private Function*.

A character called Porky co-stars with Bugs Bunny – indeed Bugs made his first appearance in 1937 in *Porky's Hare Hunt*.

Pig television stars include: popular 1960's puppets, Pinky and Perky, and Miss Piggy.

*Pig performers: Betty the pig in the award-winning film,* A Private Function *(1984), and pigs on stage in the National Theatre's production of* Animal Farm.

*Miss Piggy weighs in: self-proclaimed star of The Muppet Show, created in 1975 by Jim Henson, she is also the heroine of the 'Pigs in Space' segment featuring Dr Julius Strangepork and Link Hogthrob on their voyages in the* Swinetrek.

### Fattest Pig (USA)

A Poland–China hog, 'Big Bill': 2552 lb, 9 ft long, raised by Burford Butler of Jackson, Tennessee. Slaughtered and stuffed in 1933.

### Fattest Pig (UK)

1410 lb, 9 ft 8 ins long, owned by Joseph Lawton of Astbury, Cheshire, in 1774.

### World's Largest Litter

34, born 25–26 June 1961 in Denmark, owned by Aksel Egedee.

*This not-so-little piggy went to market: a novel form of pig transport photographed in Prachin Buri, Thailand.*

Dr Stanley E. Curtis of the Animal Science faculty of the University of Illinois has measured the decibel level of pig squeals with surprising results (in decibels):

    Average pig squeal: 100–115
    Concorde takeoff: 112

William Youatt, author of *The Pig* (1847), provides one of the most useless pig statistics ever recorded: In 1828 1,748,921 lbs of hogs' bristles were imported into Britain from Russia and Prussia. Youatt went to the trouble to calculate that this was the equivalent of 13,431,713,280 individual bristles!

The first pig to fly (right) was taken up for a $3\frac{1}{2}$ mile joyride, in a Short biplane by Lord Brabazon (holder of the first pilot's licence in Britain) on 4 November, 1909. The pig was in a basket with a sign reading: I AM THE FIRST PIG TO FLY. He didn't appear to have a choice.

I AM THE FIRST PIG TO FLY,

*(Essential reading for all porcinophiles.)*

**Blood Histamine Levels in Swine Following Total Body X-Radiation and a Flash Burn**
Hamilton A. Baxter, 1954

**The Complete Book of Bacon**
William J. Hogan, 1978

**Digestion in the Pig**
D. E. Kidder & M. J. Manners, 1978

**The Individuality of the Pig**
Robert Morrison, 1926

**Pernicious Pork; or, Astounding Revelations of the Evil Effects of Eating Swine Flesh**
William T. Hallett, 1903

**Swine in America**
Foster Dwight Coburn, 1909

**Swine Judging for Beginners**
Joel Simmonds Coffey, 1915

THE END

Acknowledgements:

Picture research by Jenny de Gex
*Cover painting (front and back) by Fred Aris,
by courtesy of The Portal Gallery*
British Library pp29, 30, 32
Curtis Brown Ltd on behalf of the Estate of
the Late Ernest Shepard p62R
Robert Estall p7
Editions Graphiques p73L
Mary Evans Picture Library pp51, 65
© Faber & Faber/British Library pp63, 64, 82
Fotomas Index pp18, 71, 72
Sally Greenhill p12
Sue Greenhill p74
Sonia Halliday Photographs pp11, 14, 33
Handmade Films p92L
© Henson Associates, 1981 from *Miss Piggy's
Guide to Life.* (Michael Joseph) p93
Michael Holford p36
Hans Jorgen Knudsen p77
Kobal Collection pp48, 56 © Hannah Barbera
Productions
© Hugh Lofting 1946,
courtesy of Jonathan Cape Ltd p61
The Mansell Collection Ltd pp9, 16, 24, 35, 39, 40
Norman Meredith by courtesy of
Chris Beetles Gallery Ltd p8R
The Museum of London p55
The National Army Museum p21
The National Theatre/
Richard Bird Graphic Designs p82R

Robert Opie Collection p54, 78
Popperfoto p26T
Private Collection p10, 26B, 53B, 53TL, 76, 78, 79
Jilliana Ranicar-Breese p53TR
Rothamsted Experimental Station p25
Royal Aeronautical Society p95
© Ronald Searle, 1973 p8L
Topham Picture Library p6, 13L, 13R, 27, 85, 86,
88, 94
Yorkshire Museum p73R
© Frederick Warne, London p62L (by permission
of the publishers)

For permission to reprint copyright material
we thank:
Oxford University Press for the extract from
*Lark Rise to Candleford* by Flora Thompson
J M Dent & Sons Ltd for the extract from
*Under Milk Wood* by Dylan Thomas
Gerald Duckworth & Co Ltd for the extract from
*The Bad Child's Book of Beasts* by Hilaire Belloc
Curtis Brown Ltd, London, on behalf of the estate of
Ogden Nash for the extract from *The Pig*
Miss D E Collins for the extract from
*The Uses of Diversity* by G K Chesterton
The trustees of Wodehouse Trust and
Century Hutchinson Ltd for the extract from
*Pig-hoo-o-o-o-ey!* by P G Wodehouse. Reprinted
by permission of the author and author's agents,
Scott Meredith Literary Agency, Inc., 845 Third
Avenue, New York, New York 10022